# FROM PROMISCUITY
## To Proverbs 31

Tanya S. Martin

*foreword* by Rev. Dr. Cynthia L. Hale

Armed & Dangerous Publishers
A Division of The Master Plan.Biz LLC
Atlanta, GA

# FROM PROMISCUITY
## To Proverbs 31

*Cover Design by C.A. SLY Designs, Atlanta, GA*

*Primary Editing by Chiquita Lockley, Atlanta, GA*
*Secondary Editing by A. Giselle Jones-Jones, Ph D. Greensboro, NC*

**From Promiscuity to Proverbs 31**
Copyright © 2005 by Tanya S. Martin
Published by Armed & Dangerous Publishers
A division of The Master Plan.Biz LLC
Atlanta, GA 30312
www.armedanddangerous.biz

ISBN 0-9777325-0-9

**Printed in the United States of America**

## Dedication

This book is dedicated to the late, **James Lankford**.

Thank you for your support and friendship and
for teaching me to live life to the fullest, to appreciate
those God has placed in my life, and to embrace love always.

It is because of your continued encouragement
and strength and your unwavering faith in God
even in your final hours that in the midst of any
storm or struggle I stand FEARLESS knowing that
God is always in control!

ACKNOWLEDGEMENTS

To my father, **Pastor Gary Martin**, who has always been my biggest cheerleader. Thank you for your tireless love and support. Thank you for training me up in the way that I should go – that I may not depart from it. Though for a season, I strayed from what I was taught, it was the Godly example and firm foundations that drew me back.

To my mother, **Debra Martin** who could have thrown in the towel when she found out at 17 that she was pregnant with me, but instead chose to give me life. I love you more than words will ever be able to express. You are my shining star, and I appreciate and adore you.

To **Ronald James**, my special gift from God. Thank you for never asking me or pressuring me to compromise on my commitment. Thank you for believing in me and accepting me for both who I am today and even who I once was. Thank you for not running from my scars and for showing me what it really means to love unconditionally.

To **Chiquita Lockley** who forced me to break up with "procrastination". She is the reason that this book is finally done. Thank you for staying on me to complete my assignment and for accepting no excuses. Thank you for being my editor. You are awesome!

To **Giselle "Moma" Jones-Jones** – You have been an inspiration in my life since day one. Thank you for not only being my mentor, but more importantly for being my friend.

To **Bishop Eddie L. Long** – Thank you for teaching me through your transparency how to be transparent myself. Thank you for every time you stepped on my toes or wounded me from the pulpit.

God used you to speak life into me and to catapult me to seek God on a level that I never knew was possible.

To **Elder Vanessa Long** - Thank you for teaching me through word and action how to be a Titus 2:3-5 and Proverbs 31 woman. You made the word tangible – brought life to the scriptures and continue to serve as an example in my life of what it means to be a Godly woman.

To **Elder Tommy Powell** and **Lady Desiree** – Thank you for sowing into my life by inviting me into yours. Your willingness to open your hearts, lives and even your marriage to me is forever appreciated. I am honored to call you friend.

To **Pastor Cynthia Hale** – You are indeed a phenomenal woman in every aspect. Thank you for raising the bar for all women across the nation. And thank you for taking the time to personally sow into my life.

And most importantly, thank you to my **Lord and Savior** who saw fit to take this messed up little girl and use me as a vessel in the Kingdom of God.

# Contents

# PART II: THE VICTORY

REVIEWS

# FROM PROMISCUITY
*To Proverbs 31*

In her book, Tanya Martin addresses the topic of *sex and sexuality inside the four walls of the church* with a transparency that is not readily available in other self-help books that are currently on the market. Not only does she share her personal pain and triumphs, but she also offers realistic suggestions for ways to maintain sexual purity in a society that does not support the notion of abstinence. This book is sure to help individuals of all ages and races confront the issues that may be blocking their victory not only in the area of sexual responsibility, but also in the areas of self-esteem, male-female relationships, friendship accountability, and more.

Chiquita Lockley,
*Author **V Is For Virgin: The Unplugged Guide To Abstinence & Celibacy***
Atlanta, GA


"From Promiscuity to Proverbs 31" is one of the rarest books you will ever read. It is truly "God Breathed." With passion, hard truth, and Holy Scripture to back up the author's words, Martin calls into account every man and woman, single or married that has lived or continues to live on the fence of sexual immorality. Martin holds your attention with her own riveting story, which evokes retrospect into ones own sexual behavior, past or present. I pray that the Lord will inspire Martin to include an accompanying journal that will serve as a catalyst for all who desire to be in the Father's will everyday of their lives.

Nanette Jones,
Certified Abstinence Educator
Canton, OH

Do you have questions about our sexually promiscuous society? If the answer is yes "From Promiscuity to Proverbs 31" is a must read. Tanya Martin's testimony is powerful, and she details how any one who is entangled in sexual sin can escape through the power of God and walk in victory. This is an easy to read book based on biblical principles that provide wisdom that will be a blessing to all!

Elder Dane T. Cunningham,
Singles Director, New Birth Missionary Baptist Church.
Lithonia, Georgia.

# FOREWORD

# FROM PROMISCUITY
## To Proverbs 31

In an age where anything goes, where people feel free to express themselves, especially sexually, Tanya Martin has had the courage to confront the issue of promiscuity in a powerful and poignant way. The promiscuity she dares to define and address is practiced among Christian singles- those of us who claim that our bodies are the Temple of the living God and yet find justification for sexual sin. In this book, the author exposes all the reasons we justify, as well as get caught up in, sexual sin.

What makes this treatise so powerful and transforming is that the author not only defines promiscuity, but she personally defines "transparency". The word transparent is from the Medieval Latin word which means "to show through" or to "show oneself". To be transparent is to be "free from pretense or deceit". Without pretense or deceit, the author tells her own story. She has allowed us to see through her own struggles and failures in this area just how destructive a lifestyle of sexual promiscuity can be. She helps the reader to see herself and the way this lifestyle can become a stronghold if "one allows one's sexual senses to be magnified, while one's resistance to sexual immorality is being desensitized."

The process of moving from Promiscuity to Proverbs 31 involves honest self-examination and openness to God. We can do this without fear because God is a God of love, grace and mercy. The process also involves understanding God's intentions when He gave us the powerful gift of sexuality.

In the same detailed and methodical way that the author analyzed the cause of failure, she shares the way to victory. Her victory can become a victory for anyone who is willing to walk the walk and not simply talk the talk. The journey from Promiscuity to Proverbs 31 is not an easy one but armed with the Word of God, one is prepared to resist the attacks of the enemy and gain and maintain self-control over one's flesh for a life of wholeness and holiness.

This book is so real and so riveting that one who has not remained pure would have to say if only I had read this book my life would have been different. And if one is still a virgin, it provides not only the motivation, but the tools by the grace of God to remain one.

**Rev. Dr. Cynthia L. Hale**
**Senior Pastor, Ray of Hope Christian Church**

PREFACE

# FROM PROMISCUITY
## To Proverbs 31

Dear Friend,

When I began writing this book, the common question was, "Who are you trying to reach?" or "Tanya, who is your target audience?" Often my answer was that I wanted to reach EVERY person - male or female, saved or unsaved - that feels trapped in sexual sin.

Because of that, I share a lot about my life in that very place. For nine years I lived a life surrounded by sexual sin in many forms; however, the seeds were sown for this lifestyle long before my first sexual encounter. That lifestyle lasted well into my early days as a Christian.

You see, for years, I lived a double life: *saved, sanctified and filled with the Holy Spirit* to my saved friends and the church members, but *"get all you can"* to my unsaved friends. And sometimes that line was blurred because I wasn't the only one giving praise to the Father on Sunday morning and seeing where I was going to "get my groove on" – Sunday night. You see, I was saved, single and sexually active.

So where is my heart? Who motivates me to be transparent and to share my story the most? The Body of Christ.

I believe that first we must break this stronghold of sexual immorality in the Body of Christ, destroying the blinders that the devil has on every Christian who feels he or she can continue living on both sides of the fence. Once the Body of Christ begins to present their bodies as a living sacrifice – holy and acceptable unto Christ – the world will be impacted and transformed.

Once we set the standard for the world instead of the world setting the standard for us – THINGS HAVE NO CHOICE BUT TO CHANGE.

I pray that this book, this journey through my past struggle with a sexually immoral lifestyle to my present victory in that area will touch the innermost parts of your heart. Allow God to speak to your specific situation, and allow Him to process all impurities from you.

Changing your lifestyle is not an overnight activity, and it won't necessarily be an easy road, but you are already equipped with everything you need to finish the process.

It can be done, and it will be done. My prayer is that every person who even thinks about picking up this book will be compelled to change his or her life and to live a life of sexual purity before God. You can't go back now if you tried because I have already prayed for you – am still praying, and will continue praying until this stronghold is non-existent.

I love you with the love of Christ. Now, here's my story ...

*Tanya S. Martin*

# INTRODUCTION

# FROM PROMISCUITY
## To Proverbs 31

(Excerpt from a journal entry)

Today, I went to the drugstore and picked up a pregnancy test because the chance that I could be with child has been heavy on my heart for the last six weeks. And although the test results were negative, it does not change the damage that has taken place in my spirit - damage much more destructive than the thought of having a child out of wedlock would ever be.

I went almost two years abstaining from sex, but in the heat of the moment, it was all thrown out the window. And I wasn't even with a man that I was in a relationship with or even a man that I cared about for that matter. He was simply a man who had crossed my path and with whom I shared a mutual sexual attraction.

Deep down inside, I don't think I ever thought it would go as far as it did that night. I mean, we had talked and shared the sexual attraction that we were feeling for each other, but it was just talk, right? At least that was what it played out to be in my mind ... that was before he came over and took me in his arms. That was before he kissed and caressed me and brought back all those feelings that had been locked away for the last two years.

I tried to say "no", - at least that is what my spirit was screaming, - but my body was speaking a completely different language as I invited him into my most sacred place. It seemed innocent enough in the beginning as we just sat together watching television; however, one kiss after another made it easy to let down all my guards. The next thing I knew, the television was watching us - watching us indulge in a sin from which I had pleaded and prayed for deliverance. A sin whose destructive web some years before had me entangled so deeply that I never thought I would be able to escape. Now here I am, back at square one asking myself again, "How did I get to this place?"

So Tanya, how did you get back to this place? How is it that you were able to abstain from sexual immorality while in a relationship, but you failed the test with a man to whom you had no ties? In the days following that night, those were just a few of the many questions that plagued me.

There are many things that I've come to realize about this "place" – the most obvious to me today is that I had gotten so caught up in the amount of time that I had abstained, that I had lost focus of why I was abstaining to begin with. It was no longer about keeping God's mandate to flee fornication, but it became more about how long Tanya (the person, in flesh) could maintain. I was setting myself up to fail, which I ultimately did. I engaged in a conversation that I knew I was not able to handle. In my past, I had talked a good game, but my actions always backed up my talk. So why is it that I thought it appropriate to talk the talk and think I wouldn't have to or want to back it up with the action to prove that I was more than just talk?

These are the surface things that were taking place in my life, but I realize that it is so much more important for me to dig deeper into what was really taking place. I had not totally surrendered to God's will in this matter. Although for two years, my outward interactions with men did not display sexual immorality, I had indulged personally in many ways. My thoughts alone were like the chapters of an erotic love story where nothing was forbidden. My mind was still in bondage to a stronghold that kept me from walking in total victory in this area.

Today I am more determined than ever to walk in holiness and in purity. I have rationed out pieces of myself to man after man since my first sexual encounter in 1993. I have unwrapped and given away a gift that God intended for my husband. And though I cannot get the original gift back, I know that my God is a restorer. I want to be whole again – I want to reclaim all of Tanya that I once gave away. I want to love myself like I've never loved myself before. I want to be holy, as God is holy. At all costs – I will continue to stand. Even if that means that I have to stand by myself. I realize that this commitment means I have to exercise a higher level of self control, and I have to raise the standards in every area of my life. I realize that the crucifying of my flesh must be a daily task. And though I know it won't be an easy journey, I stand knowing that I am more than a conqueror, and that God has already equipped me with everything that I need for the fight.

If sharing my story from the beginning will keep another person from making the destructive choices that I have made, I vow to be transparent and share it. I will not be ashamed because while it's true I've done the things that I will write about, I am no longer that person. God has forgiven me and purged me from all unrighteousness. And He qualified me for such a time as this. I am armed with the word of God and knowledge of who He has called me to be, which makes me a dangerous threat to the devil and all who stand with him.

# FROM PROMISCUITY
*To Proverbs 31*

## pro·mis·cu·ous
*adj.*

1. Having casual sexual relations frequently with different partners; indiscriminate in the choice of sexual partners.
2. Not restricted to one sexual partner.
3. Lacking standards of selection; indiscriminate.
4. Casual; random.

## DISCLAIMER:

**No one having sex outside of the confines of a marriage covenant is exempt from being called promiscuous. If the person with whom you are having a sexual relationship is not your spouse – definition #4 fits – for you are having casual sex.**

# PART I

## THE STRUGGLE

# CHAPTER 1: BACK TO THE BEGINNING

*Low Self~Esteem: The Root of Self Destruction*

"Hey Skinny Minnie!"
"You are so bony!"
"Do you ever eat? Are you anorexic?"
"My God, you are so tiny –
looks like someone could break you in half."

For many years, these were the kinds of statements with which family, friends, classmates, teachers, church members and even strangers greeted me. The comments seemed irrelevant, and most people didn't mean any harm; however, those words were shaping who I was and what I thought of myself. I became very self-conscious of my size, and although I had a "pretty face", I thought I was ugly. My self-image didn't stand a chance against the harsh criticism that was forming in my heart and mind, especially during adolescence when boys starting paying attention to girls. How would I ever get any attention if, when they looked at me, all they saw and thought was *skinny minnie, bones, slim, stick girl?* I remember asking myself, "Who would ever find me 'sexy' if all they thought when they saw me was 'bony'?" It was an issue that I cried about in the middle of the night when no one was around to hear my cries. I kept a smile on my face even though the hurt and fear of *lack of acceptance* was burning a hole in my heart.

Over the years, I don't think I ever thought of myself as a person who suffered from "self-esteem" issues. Many of us don't. When people refer to someone as having low respect for themselves, we have been trained to have a pigeon-hole perspective of what that looks like. We picture the boy with the trifocals or the girl with the braces and really bad skin. Or what about the little chubby girl that everyone makes fun of in the cafeteria or that really poor family at the end of the block? Surely they all suffer with this problem. And who knows, perhaps they do, but I guarantee you that they are not the only ones suffering. I know many homecoming and prom queens that suffered from low "self-esteem", and many rich and famous people that suffered from it as well. This issue is no respecter of persons, and it will attach itself to whomever it desires.

**self-es·teem**

n.

Pride in oneself; self-respect.

For me, I didn't necessarily fit the description of a person with low self esteem. I had an outgoing personality, made excellent grades, and hung with the "in" crowds at school. But none of that mattered because I didn't take pride in myself, and my actions later in life proved that I didn't have self-respect. From high school on, I've always been quite the center of attention, surrounded by friends and always involved in some group, activity, or function. But as I truly re-examine my past, I see that this ugly spirit reared its head in my life a little differently than what we are typically accustomed to hearing about. For that reason it went unnoticed ...and my story may be similar to yours.

So yes, I grew up with "self-esteem" issues that I never classified as such, and it wasn't until I tried to trace back to the source of my sexually immoral lifestyle, that the root (low self esteem) of the problem surfaced. I didn't fit the "profile" of a promiscuous girl, at least not by the labels most associated to them in society. Often, society would have us make the assumption that all women that are promiscuous grew up in a home where their father was not present, or if he was physically present, there wasn't a good relationship between the two. However, that is not my story. My father played a major role in my life and affirmed me regularly. So my problem didn't stem from trying to fill a "father" void, which is why it took me a while to trace the problem back to its true roots.  Plus, I never would have labeled myself as promiscuous because that was only for the girls who slept with a whole lot of men ...Or so I thought, but as the disclaimer for this book states: **No one having sex outside of the confines of a marriage covenant is exempt from being called promiscuous.  If the person with whom you are having a sexual relationship is not your spouse – definition #4 below fits – for you are having casual sex.**

So why did my life take the course that it did?  Why did I find myself in sexual relationship after sexual relationship?  Why was I promiscuous?  Well, it stemmed from a "self-esteem" issue, but one that no one ever knew even existed.  It came from an issue that I didn't even realize had taken such a toll on my life and my outlook of myself.  The seeds were sown as a child when I was ashamed and embarrassed by what I thought was negative attention of my size.  Then, the seeds were watered by my attempts to change how people – men in particular, looked at me.

As a child, I was cruelly picked on because of my size ... as I grew older, I did get more attention from men, but this attention stemmed from the fact that I was extremely flirty, and still a virgin.  Looking back, I realize that for many of those guys, I was a challenge, and they just wanted to be the one to "break me in."  They wanted the credit of being my first sexual experience, but, I had made a standard for myself, I was not having sex before I graduated from high school.  As you see my standards were not very high.  I never even desired to wait until I was married.  I just didn't want to have a child while in high school because I knew how my mother had struggled by having me at 17.  So while I prided myself in graduating as a virgin, it wouldn't be long after graduation that I would lose my virginity.  At that time, losing that part of myself wasn't an issue because I had accomplished my only goal as it related to my sexual encounters ... graduating as a virgin.  Now imagine what course my life could have taken if I had set higher standards. It took dedication and commitment to make it to graduation when everyone around me was having sex. If I had maintained that level of commitment, I know I could have stayed a virgin until marriage - but I had set my standard too low. What standards have you set for your life? Perhaps, they are too low like mine were, but it's not too late to raise the bar! Won't you reexamine your standards and reset them by the Word of God instead of by the world's standard?

I graduated in June of 1992, and it wasn't until the fall of 1993 that I lost (no, I gave away) my virginity. In the meantime, I experimented with coming as close to the fire as possible without actually getting burnt. I no longer had boundaries set for what I would and would not do on a date, so it was just a matter of time before I would find myself caught up. Once men began to respond to me sexually, for the first time I thought I was really beautiful. Sex became my control mechanism - at least I thought it gave me control. So I began to allow it to rule my life, thinking that if I turned a man out in bed, he would always be there for me. It no longer mattered that I was "skinny", because in the bedroom, I felt "sexy" – finally.

Low "self-esteem" has become the subject of many conversations, discussions and debates on why children choose to take the wrong paths. We look at troubled teens, and we try to pinpoint what it is about them that bring them insecurities. Is it a long pointed nose? Is it an awkward shaped figure? Perhaps it's a freckled face, or is it the texture of the hair? Does she think that she is overweight? Does he have a complex because he is the shortest guy in class? These are the questions that we link with destructive behavior.

Then when we take the focus off of physical features, we look for the emotional scars. We dissect every possible scenario that could have caused them to have low "self-esteem". Perhaps their parents were separated. Maybe they grew up in an abusive household. Maybe no one ever told them they were loved. When they look in the mirror, maybe they don't like the image that they see reflected back to them. It's true that a low sense of self worth can destroy one's self image. Yes, it is true that if one doesn't feel validated he or she may look to all the wrong forces seeking that validation. And any person dealing with low "self-esteem" issues needs to get to the root of the problem and allow God to work it out in their lives. But many times, as we categorize those who we think are struggling with this problem, we leave out a whole class of people who also suffer.

There are many boys and girls, men and women who have a major battle with self worth, yet we look right over them. We look past them because from the outside looking in, they appear to have it all together. You know the story: they grew up with both of their parents, people generally find them attractive, they are smart and get good grades, may even be captain of the cheerleading squad or the football team. They have you fooled, and many even have themselves fooled because they walk around with a smile on their face as if they are sitting on top of the world, when in actuality, they are broken inside.

When they are alone with themselves, the truth begins to surface and the lack of value they have of themselves becomes obvious through the choices that they make. They allow people to mistreat them and degrade them, sometimes in the most subtle ways. The truth of the matter is that they are having an internal struggle with something that probably no one else knows about. So while you are writing them off as the poster child for having it all together, they are dying inside. This is the life of many people who find themselves caught in sexual immorality. That was my story.

We have to be careful not to limit the *symptoms* of low "self-esteem" because when we do, many people continue to suffer from it. No one allows them to deal with their very real issues. Don't believe that just because things look okay that your children, your friends, your co-workers, your neighbors, or those with whom you labor in ministry are not struggling with some of the same issues. It may not be the thing that seems most obvious; as a matter of fact, many times it is not. As responsible Christians, we have to pull off the layers to get to the root of the real problem.

Many of the things we see that dishearten us (i.e., the women in rap music videos, the revealing clothes that women are wearing, men with their pants hanging down, children defying their parents, married people in adulterous relationships) stem from "self-esteem" issues that were never dealt with. These symptoms are just the result of a deeper problem. In some cases, people don't even know that a problem exists, so we try to fight the result without pulling out the root. We may solve a temporary problem, but it is destined to resurface in another form if we don't reconstruct from the foundation first.

Many of you are experiencing or have experienced the same thing. You are trying to cover up a body complex or area of low "self-esteem" by allowing people to have their way with you. You think that you will be considered more attractive if you give in to their sexual needs. You seek validation from the opposite sex by any means necessary. You lack respect and pride in yourself because you were never taught how to love yourself. It's time to embrace who you are, and to realize that we are all, *fearfully and wonderfully made* (Psalm 139:14).

For you, maybe it's no longer the physical things that bring a lowered "self-esteem", but rather in your case, it may be your self-worth as a whole. For whatever reason, you don't feel like you are good enough. You think that you don't deserve or just never will have a person that will treat you the way you should be treated, so you settle for whoever comes along. Or you do things just to have someone in your life. These situations may sound foolish and immature, but there are Christians who are battling in this way even after years of being saved. For some, they think they've done too much dirt to change now. We are all guilty of making some jacked up decisions in our lives, but God commissions us in Isaiah 43:18 *not to remember the former things, nor to consider the things of old, for behold, He is doing a new thing. It shall spring forth, shall you not know it.* He is asking us if we can perceive it. Can we embrace it? Or are we going to continue walking around with a "woe is me" mindset stuck in what happened yesterday?

Others feel they are not "holy" enough for a pure relationship, but they fail to realize that holiness is an on-going process. Purity doesn't happen overnight and your past does not disqualify you. Some wonder what they have to bring to the table if not sex. Basically, it all comes down to not knowing who you are in Christ. Once you know who you are, you will realize that YOU are the best thing you could ever bring to the table. You don't have to turn tricks to keep him or her there with you. If you have to do this, that's not where you need to be anyway.

Are you still not convinced of how valuable you really are? One of the first steps in destroying the yoke of low self esteem is to combat it with scriptures of who you are in Christ. It doesn't matter what anyone else thinks or what they may have called you. What does God say about you? You should take the time to load up on ammunition by finding as many scriptures as possible that will remind you of what God says about you. Here are a few of the things He says:

~~~~~~~~~~~~~~~~~~~~~~~~~~~~~~~~~~~~~~~~~~~

### I Peter 2:9

But you are a chosen generation, a royal priesthood, a holy nation, His own special people, that you may proclaim the praises of Him who called you out of darkness into His marvelous light.

### Jeremiah 1:5
Before I formed you in the womb I knew you; Before you were born I sanctified you; I ordained you a prophet to the nations.

### Jeremiah 29:11
For I know the thoughts that I think toward you, says the Lord, thoughts of peace and not of evil, to give you a future and a hope.

### Philippians 4:13
I can do all things through Christ who strengthens me.

### Deuteronomy 28:13
And the Lord will make you the head and not the tail; you shall be above only, and not beneath, if you heed the commandments of the Lord your God, which I command you today, and are careful to observe them.

*Life and death are in the power of the tongue.* Speak life always. Once we get a grasp on who God says we are and we ARM ourselves with that knowledge, we become a DANGEROUS threat to the enemy because he can no longer deceive us by attacking our self esteem. People can't validate you; only God can do that. And He does just that over and over again in scripture. You must saturate your spirit, your mind, and your heart with those scriptures. Keep studying them and meditating on them until you really believe what they say. You will find that when you truly believe that you are priceless, there are certain situations and certain circumstances to which you will no longer fall victim. You must really believe that your body is a temple so that you won't defile it. This belief will help you begin the process of cutting out sexually immoral acts. You have to remind yourself that we serve a forgiving God who knows everything that we have done, yet is always willing to wipe the slate clean. Often times, we are stuck in bondage not because God has not forgiven us, but rather because we have not forgiven ourselves. We can't accept God's grace and mercy nor his blessings and promises because we don't think we deserve them. However, God tells us in Isaiah 43:1b to *"Fear not, for I have redeemed you; I have called you by your name. You are mine."* It's time that we walk in that redemption.

Today at 31, I am no bigger than I was in high school, and though sometimes I still get the "skinny minny" comments, they no longer bother me. I know that I was formed and fashioned by God's hand. When he created me, he created a beautiful person – inside and out, and I am free from the condemning power of people's opinions and comments. I have accepted God's forgiveness for my past mistakes, and I have forgiven myself. Over the years, as I continued to study the scriptures of who I am in Christ, that issue of low self esteem was eliminated in my life, and now the devil can no longer attack me there. I also tackled the enormous task of facing my past – looking it right in the eye. So if someone tries to bring it up and throw it in my face, I don't have to go run under the guilt and shame rock. Instead, I can boldly declare that *God has blotted out my transgressions, washed me thoroughly from my iniquity, and cleansed me from all of my sins. He has purged me with hyssop so that I may be clean and washed me that I may be whiter than snow* (Psalm 51). Simply put, God took my past life of sin and washed the slate clean, giving me the opportunity to start over again. What will you say when the enemy tries to attack you? Will you tell him that God has given you a clean slate as well? How will you combat your issues of low self-esteem? Tell me my friend, what does God say about you? Remember, it is not what name people call you, but what name you answer to that matters. Learn to love yourself in spite of any flaws that you believe you have. God created us each with a unique design. Embrace it because God does not make mistakes.

# CHAPTER 2: PROSTITUTION
## *Not Just A Street Mentality*

# FROM PROMISCUITY
## To Proverbs 31

God what do you mean that I am just like the prostitute selling her body on the street? How can you compare me with the hooker on the corner? Surely my actions don't look like the woman with the low cut, see-thru blouse, black leather mini-skirt and stilettos; the one working the midnight hours on the strip, flagging down any man she can in hopes of making enough money to pay her bills or to foot her drug habit.

No God – you got it all wrong – he is not my pimp, and I definitely am NOT a prostitute! I am not having sex for money. Yes, he buys me new clothes. Yes, he pays my rent and car note. Yes, I know that I can get anything I want from him as long as the sexual favors continue to come, but he doesn't control me. He is definitely not pimping me!

Yes God, my relationship with him is based on sex alone and no, he is not my husband. But I, the pastor's daughter – the one who's been in church her whole life -prostituting my body? Don't you think that is a little extreme?

Like most others, I had an image of what I thought pimps and prostitutes looked like. That is until God showed me how I was prostituting my body every time I laid down with any man who was not my husband. No, I wasn't on the corner selling my body, but I was having sex in exchange for something else. And I was definitely having sex outside of the confines of a marriage covenant. I clearly knew what the Bible said about fornication; but for whatever reason, I thought I was exempt. For some reason, I felt justified to have sex because of all the things I did "right." Surely I could have a pass for this one sin, right? Plus, everyone was having sex, so what was the big deal? At least that is what I kept telling myself. There was really no level of guilt or shame about my actions leading up to the *prostitution* revelation God gave me. During this period of my life, I had no intentions of stopping; therefore, I never really repented for my sexual sins.

To me, having sex was a very minor sin that wasn't hurting me or anyone else. I believed that when the time came for me to stop, I could just turn it on and off. When the day came, and I made the decision to commit to abstinence it would be a done deal because, you know ... it was just sex ...no biggie. But just like many drug addicts who start off with something that seems minor (like smoking weed) and once they've conquered that high, search for a greater high, I too experimented with levels of sexual activity. Okay – so sex just to be having sex had been great, but I knew there was something bigger than that. So it then became a situation of *what could I get* in return for sexual favors? Although I never actually SPOKE those words, the choices I made for my life reflected that attitude and mentality.

You see for me, my next move was what the world calls a "sugar daddy" relationship. At the age of 20, I met and began sleeping with a man 15 years older who introduced me to a whole new dimension of sexuality. I was with him not because I loved him, but simply because he was providing me with a lifestyle that I had never experienced - luxury home, luxury car, shopping sprees, exotic vacations, weekly hair appointments, manicures, pedicures and facials ... Do you get the picture? He met my every need as long as I met his every sexual desire. In many ways, I had made him my God because whenever I needed anything, I expected him to solve my problem and meet my need. And that was exactly what he did for a couple of years.

This relationship was very emotionally and verbally abusive. You see, I had given this man control of my body so it was only a matter of time before he gained control of my mind as well. He knew that he held a certain level of power over me because I was now caught up in the lifestyle of having anything I wanted – anytime I wanted it. There was nothing that I couldn't ask him for and he not provide it. Yes, in many ways he had become my pimp. This control and power set the course for the next 7 or 8 years of my life.

Whenever I didn't "act" right according to the rules set by my "sugar daddy," he would say things like "the only thing you are good for is sex." And when I threatened to leave, he would tell me that no man would ever want me because I was "used up." So you're asking, why did I stay around? I stayed because I cared more about the material things I was attaining than I did about myself. I, the honor student who had graduated at the top of my high school class and on my way to graduating at the top of my college class, was not thinking clearly in this predicament. I even left college and moved from Kentucky to North Carolina to be closer to him. Yes, I was caught up. But it took only one night of the emotional and verbal abuse to turn physical for this young girl to wake up and realize that I was in a bad situation. So I took flight and began my plan of escape from him.

Though I left that situation, I took a lot of baggage from it with me – including his famous words that *all I had to offer anyone was my body.* And though I denied that accusation, it had begun to take root in my spirit. Over the years to come, I would begin to act out and become the very thing he said I was. I was looking for love, but settling for a mere temporary sexual satisfaction. Again and again. You see, baggage is a very powerful thing because many of us don't even acknowledge the fact that we have it. We may wonder why we respond to certain situations the way we do or why we keep getting caught in the same predicaments, but we never want to admit that we may be carrying some excess baggage. Until you deal with that baggage you're carrying, you will continue to be destroyed by it. We must "unpack" our bags.

It was also through this relationship that I began to understand the strength of a sexual tie or stronghold. One would think that once I got out of that relationship, I would never look back, but such was not the case. Two or three years later, I let my guard down and accepted his phone call. He called to apologize and told me how he knew that I was a wonderful woman and that he just wanted to at least salvage a friendship. Did I really think we could be friends? He wasn't my friend when we were together. He was my pimp. So why was I foolish enough to open any door for him to come back into my life? Who knows, but I did just that. By opening that door, I allowed myself to be entangled again with that yoke of bondage. Soul ties will make you do things you said you would never do.

**Galatians 5:1**
Stand fast therefore in the liberty by which
Christ has made us free, and do not be entangled
again with a yoke of bondage.

When I left the relationship, I went back to college, but when money got tight as a student, I knew I could always rely on him to relieve the stress. The difference was that by this point I thought I was the one in control, the one calling the shots. My voice mail picked up whenever he called me, but I availed myself to him when I needed something. Regardless of what I thought, I was not in control. He was still my pimp, and I was still his prostitute. And not just his, but every other man with whom I had a sexual relationship. Even if I wasn't getting material things in return, God showed me that I was still prostituting my body. And for what? Affirmation? Affection? Twisted love? Some warped sense of security?

I can just imagine what you are thinking right now because I probably thought the same thing. Let's see. Are you thinking – "Ok Tanya, that might have been your story, but I am not a prostitute."

41

# FROM PROMISCUITY
*To Proverbs 31*

Believe me, I understand, that "prostitute" is a title no one wants. I remember after my first conversation with God about it, I drove into the inner city to places where prostitutes were known to frequent. As I drove down the street, I was shouting ... "See God, now that is a prostitute! Not me." I remember watching movies and pointing out, "Now she is a prostitute, and he is a pimp ... Not me!" But God made it plain for me, so let me do the same for you. Let's take a closer look, clear the air, and clarify some things.

Webster defines **prostitute** as:

1. One who solicits and accepts payment for sex acts.
2. One who sells one's abilities, talent,
or name for an unworthy purpose.

*Do you still deny that your
actions line up with that definition?*

*Well, tell me what has been the purpose
of you indulging in sexual immorality?*

*What "payments" have you
received in exchange for sex?*

*Why are you having sex outside of marriage?*

The first barrier we have to overcome is our notion of "payment." Of course, we instantly think of a monetary exchange, but in this case a payment does not necessarily have to be money. Just like some prostitutes on the street get paid by drugs, some of us get paid by clothes, dinners, the ballet, or get this - the security of being called the significant other. Yes sir, yes ma'am – some of us have fallen victim to having sex simply to keep a man or to keep a woman. In essence, your "payment" is the relationship.

The second barrier to overcome is our ideal of an "unworthy purpose." *Unworthy means that it is insufficient in worth, lacks value, not suiting or befitting.* You may be like me and spend a lot of time justifying your sexual sin. You may even believe since you are in love with this person and plan to marry him or her that it makes it okay. Well, I have an important news flash for you. Simply put, if what you are doing does not line up with God's original intention, plan and purpose for sex, then it automatically defaults to an unworthy purpose.

This truth is a hard thing to swallow. I understand because I know it was tough for me. We live in a society where sex is constantly *in your face,* making it much easier to just follow suit and play the sex game. Think about it. You can't listen to the radio for more than 10 minutes before a song comes on talking about sex. You can't look at television without the commercials being filled with sexual overtones. And the majority of the movies that come out start with a sex scene. Sex was not designed to be used as a tool to sell songs, products, movies or ourselves; however, that is the cycle in which we have allowed ourselves to become trapped.

But there is hope. Yes, we are guilty of the acts that we committed, but thankfully, we serve a forgiving God. He simply wants us to repent (turn away) from those sins and live a life that is pleasing to Him. I Corinthians 6:9-11 tells us that *the unrighteous will not inherit the Kingdom of God.* The "unrighteous" includes fornicators. Notice in verse 11 it says, *"And such <u>were</u> some of you. <u>But</u> you were washed, but you were sanctified, but you were justified in the name of the Lord Jesus and by the Spirit of our God."* This verse lets us know that it is never too late to get it right with God.

We don't have to walk around in condemnation to the life we have lived. We cannot allow the enemy to convince us that we are "used" up and not qualified to be forgiven. We can destroy the yokes and strongholds of our past, leave the "baggage" we have accumulated at the door and not take it into our next relationship. We are equipped to carry out the mandate in I Thessalonians 4:3-7 which says: *For this is the will of God, your sanctification: that you should abstain from sexual immorality; that each of you should know how to **possess his own vessel in sanctification and honor,** not in passion of lust, like the Gentiles who do not know God.*

The Bible is clear that we are not to fornicate. God goes as far as to say in I Corinthians 6:18 to *flee fornication.* "Flee" means to run away, to pass swiftly, to vanish. The intensity of that command lets us know how serious God is about sexual immorality. Don't fall victim to prostitution another day. Take a stand and present your body *holy and acceptable* unto God. Remember, our bodies don't belong to us anyway. I Corinthians 6:19 says, *Or do you not know that your body is the temple of the Holy Spirit who is in you, whom you have from God, and you are not your own.* Therefore, we need to show more respect by honoring them and presenting them as the instruments of righteousness that they were designed to be.

# CHAPTER 3: PORNOGRAPHY & MASTURBATION
*Our Senses Magnified ~ Our Values Desensitized*

# FROM PROMISCUITY
## To Proverbs 31

It's 7:21AM on a Sunday morning, and the praise team is singing one of my favorite songs. The Holy Spirit is moving mightily, and I am totally surrendered to God –standing in complete expectation for Him to move in a way that only He can. My hands are raised, and I am singing a new song unto the Lord, when all of a sudden, I can no longer hear the voices of the praise team or even those standing around me. No longer am I singing, "Praise Is What I Do." Instead, there is an exotic sex scene from a movie I saw years ago, replaying in my head - every intricate detail, clear as day – almost as if I made the movie myself ...*TURN THAT OFF. Click, click – station changed ...Oh my, look at his triceps and biceps and ...umm ... he is absolutely delicious. It doesn't make any sense for Morris Chestnut to be so incredibly beautiful. Yeah, I know he is married, but ouuuhh wee – if I .... TURN THAT OFF. Click, click – station changed – It's that latest video that everyone has been talking about... what did they just say? He wants to do what to her what? And he wants to do it where? What? He wants to share with his boys? What in the He\*@! TURN THAT MESS OFF. Click, click...So what do we have here? ... That looks like my house ... my bedroom. Okay, okay, here we go – this has to be more appropriate viewing for my Christian eyes ... it's a little dim in here though. Is that good old, classic Marvin Gaye playing in the background? Where am I? What is this? Oh wait – that's no movie anymore, or half naked picture. It's not even a music video clip – Is that me? Please don't tell me that is me and ... Why is my mind taking me back there? ... Yes, it was hot and steamy –One for the record books – BUT - WHO IN THE WORLD PUSHED PLAY on the mental video recorder and why in the world would you play the tape during worship service?*

Then a little voice says to me, "Didn't you know, Tanya, that the impressions made in your mind are no respecter of persons or places? We will take you back to that former place any chance we get. And we have plenty of things from which to choose to replay for you. No, you might not subscribe to *Playboy* or *Hustler*. You don't even rent pornographic videos, but you love those erotica novels. You watch hours of late night music videos, and you have indulged in your share of sexual exploration. Unfortunately for you, hard core porn, soft porn, raunchy videos, nude pictures, erotica novels, and sometimes even regular prime time television all carry sex as their recurring themes. They all leave irrevocable impressions in your mind, but even worse, indentions on your spirit. Over the years, your "sexual" senses have continued to be magnified while your resistance to sexual immorality has been desensitized. So you continue to take in more and more and then when you least expect it, the sin creeps right back to the forefront of your thoughts. And here you were in praise and worship – thinking you were surrendering yourself to God. But ... we **GOTCHA** ...AGAIN."

Have you been there? You know, minding your own business but getting caught up in a flashback. Maybe it didn't happen in the middle of Sunday morning service like my situation. Maybe you were at dinner with the man or woman of your dreams when all of a sudden you were remembering the last person you slept with, or the last pornographic movie or magazine you saw, your late night surfing on the **XXX** internet sites or perhaps the last time you took matters into your own hands and decided to masturbate. Whatever the case may be for you, there is "video footage" stored away for what I call the moment of the "broken video player." It typically occurs out of the blue with no prior warning. One moment everything is flowing like your typical day, and then it's as if someone pushed play on the VCR and a clip of a previous sexual encounter, or a recap of a pornographic movie you watched or a pornographic magazine you flipped through, or what you did last night when you were alone in your room in the wee hours of the night, **BEAMS** across the big screen of your mind. I call it the BROKEN video player because although you immediately try to turn it off – it won't go away. You didn't ask for this to become a fresh memory in your thoughts, but unfortunately when we sow seeds we don't have control over when the harvest will spring forth.

Everyone has his or her own story of how things unfolded in his or her world. I've talked to men who stumbled upon their father's or uncle's *Playboy* collection as a young child. Though they thought it innocent to flip through the magazine, seeds were sown, and the roots of addiction began at that very early and tender age. As they got older, they snuck around to get their hands on more and more porn. Some even got married, and though they had a beautiful wife beside them who was everything they every imagined in a woman, they still had to get a daily or weekly "fix" of porn. I know women who in the journey of abstinence were encouraged by their friends, family and even doctors that masturbation was normal, a way to release sexual tension – a substitute for sex ... a way to escape fornication. So you find yourself asking the question, "Is there really anything wrong with this? Does the Bible tell us not to indulge in pornography or masturbation?"

For years, I tried to find a clear cut answer for that question. The scriptures are clear for us about fornication – as we know, it says in I Corinthians 6:18 *to flee fornication.* So, we don't have to draw our own conclusions on what God thinks about fornication. Pornography and Masturbation are not as clear cut. I agree with this argument, for I have not found a scripture that says, *Thou shalt not indulge in pornography or masturbation, or else you will surely die.* But perhaps, we just need to look at the scripture a little more in-depth. Let's examine what happens while we indulge and the aftermath of indulging.

In order for us to successfully explore this topic together, I believe that it is important for us to be on one accord.

*Can we agree that it is our flesh and not our spirit that desires fornication, pornography and masturbation?*

*Can we agree that the more we indulge, the more addictive it becomes, thus causing us to want it even more?*

*Can we agree that when we are engaged in these activities that our minds and thoughts are not geared towards Christ, but instead they are geared towards some form of self-gratification?*

*Can we agree that our minds and our spirits are constantly in war with each other, and that we have to decide which one controls our actions?*

**"Pornography (Naked Pictures)**
is visual rape that strips the body of its beauty and innocence resulting in lust and degradation."
– T. Martin

When one looks at pornography or practices masturbation, are they not engaged in inappropriate sexual activity – even if it's only in their minds? Let's start with pornography. The majority of pornography is what? ... Random couples indulging in some form of sexual activity? Tell me - are they not fornicating? If we are not to engage in fornication, why would it be okay to watch it? And what happened to the original plan of sex being a form of worship between a husband and wife? Pornography cheapens the act to simply a means for one to release his or her sexual tension. What had been created and ordained for the sacred confines of marriage has now become a common commodity. What porn video have you ever watched that glorified God? What glory does God get when you have an orgy taking place on your television screen? Or a man being beat like he is some wild animal? Or a woman being called a bi*@# or whore while she is performing sexual favors?

Indulging in any level of pornography opens up the door for the devil to come in and wreak havoc. One can become very sensitive to the mere sight of skin. And in today's society where naked skin is readily available in the videos, prime time sitcoms, movies and unfortunately sometimes right on the pew beside you in the sanctuary, you find yourself on high alert and sexually aroused on a regular basis. Not only that, but pornography along with other sexual sins such as masturbation feed the flesh, which in turn tightens the grip that sexual immorality has on the mind.

~~~~~~~~~~~~~~~~~~~~~~~~~~~~

**"Pornography (Sexual Acts)**

is the public display and humiliation of
God-ordained, private, intimate moments created
for the confines of a marriage covenant."
– T. Martin

~~~~~~~~~~~~~~~~~~~~~~~~~~~~

Ok, so you say "no" to pornography and you choose to just masturbate instead because at least now you are not engaging in fornication nor are you watching someone else fornicate. So why do you masturbate? Because it feels good? Just because it feels good does not make it good for you. I Corinthians 6:12 says, *All things are lawful for me, but all things are not helpful. All things are lawful for me, but I will not be brought under the power of any.* Is there not a level of addiction that results with regular engagement of masturbation? Furthermore, when you masturbate, do you not achieve the same level or a substitution for the climax that occurs during sexual intercourse? If the Word tells us not to fornicate, I don't believe it is giving us permission to achieve the same thing through alternative means. When God created sex, I believe that he knew how incredible it would be, how good it would make us feel, and the power of the climax. He ordained for us to experience that climax through sex between a husband and a wife only. When one masturbates, or as we sometimes call it "taking matters into our own hands," he or she steps in and tries to be God, coming up with a new way of achieving what God sanctioned only for marriage.

Let's go back to the war between our mind and our spirit. When you masturbate, are you not feeding your lustful thoughts and desires? What are you thinking about while masturbating? In Philippians 4:8, the word tells us to *think on things that are true, noble, just, **pure**, lovely, of good report and things that are of virtue and praiseworthy.* Let's just look at the word "pure" for a moment. Webster defines pure as:

1. Having a homogeneous or uniform composition; not mixed
2. Free from adulterants or impurities
3. Free of dirt, defilement, or pollution
4. Free of foreign elements
5. Containing nothing inappropriate or extraneous
6. Complete; utter
7. Having no faults; sinless
8. Chaste; virgin

The first definition is *having a homogenous or uniform composition* – not mixed. This definition took me back to James 3:11 where it asks the question, *"Does a spring send forth fresh water and bitter from the same opening?* Can one glorify God with their temple while they are glorifying flesh and their lustful desires at the same time? No, that is not possible. Purity and sin do not mix.

They are not homogenous. One cannot walk in the spirit and in the flesh simultaneously. Galatians 5:16 -17 says, *Walk in the Spirit, and you shall not fulfill the lust of the flesh. For the flesh lust against the Spirit, and the Spirit against the flesh; and these are contrary to one another, so that you do not do the things you wish.* Romans 8:5-6 says, *For those who live according to the flesh set their minds on the things of the flesh, but those who live according to the Spirit, the things of the Spirit. For to be carnally (fleshly) minded is death, but to be spiritually minded is life and peace.*

I had a guy friend who was trying to abstain from sex, yet he would go to the strip club on a regular basis. He couldn't understand why abstinence was so hard for him. He was feeding his flesh, and whatever you feed will flourish. You cannot position yourself in sexual situations and expect flesh not to crave more of it. After a while, the pornography, strip clubs, masturbation, etc. will get old to you, and you will seek a greater high ... the real thing. Let's not fool ourselves into thinking that indulging in these activities are solutions to the struggle. Aside from the fact that these activities are simply not fitting for a saint, they actually make the struggle harder. Straddling the fence is like someone on a diet buying a bag of chocolate chip cookies and saying, "I am just going to look at them, maybe hold them in my hand – but I vow to refrain from eating them." Sounds foolish right? So what is the difference in you saying, "I am just going to touch myself to keep from letting someone else touch me?" Or "I am not going to have sex, but I will just watch someone else have sex." Again ... FOOLISH thinking.

> "**Masturbation**
> eliminates the beauty of arousal and climax
> between a husband and wife by attempting to
> capture that moment through self inflicted resources."
> - T. Martin

So you have engaged in masturbation and/or pornography and may have even been a victim of the broken video player, what do you do now? It's time to begin the process of "taping over" what has been recorded in your memory and in your spirit. Go back to Philippians 4:8 and begin to think on those things in that scripture. Pray for crop failure for those seeds that were sown. Indulge in things that feed and nourish your spirit man instead of your flesh. Romans 6:18 lets us know that *we can be set free from sin and become slaves of righteousness.*

We cannot erase the past or erase the fact that we have allowed impurities and contamination to infiltrate our lives, but it's never to late for a fresh start. This start does, however, require action on our part. It's not good enough to say, "I am standing in faith that God is going to remove these desires from me." No – faith is an **action word**, which means making some practical moves. Destroy the pornography in your house. Delete those websites from your favorites links on your computer. Interrupt those lustful thoughts by praying as soon as they enter your mind. Watch the content of your conversations when you are hanging out with your friends. Romans 12:9b says, *Abhor what is evil. Cling to what is good.* "Abhor" means *to detest, to regard with horror or loathing.* These are very strong words, but that lets us know how strong we need to stand against sinful ways.

Romans 13: 14 says to *put on the Lord Jesus Christ and*

*make no provision for the flesh, to fulfill its lusts.* Each of us is different, and we all have our weak moments. Identify what your weak moments are, and make sure you do everything you can to avoid those moments. If seeing a sex scene in a regular movie causes your mind to go to that place where later you will find yourself engaging in masturbation or pornography – don't watch that movie. Make **NO PROVISION** for flesh. This means that sometimes you have to make extreme sacrifices. You can't listen to everything nor can you watch everything. Your appetite for masturbation and pornography did not appear overnight so more than likely, your deliverance won't either. Continue to actively crucify your flesh daily. Continue to pray, setting your mind and thoughts on Godly things. Don't be discouraged but continue to press on. *Do not grow weary while doing good, for in due season, you shall reap if you do not lose heart (Galatians 6:9).*

# CHAPTER 4: CYCLES OF DESTRUCTION

*Searching For Love, Settling For Lust*

# FROM PROMISCUITY
## To Proverbs 31

### Monday morning
(me to one of my girlfriends):

"Oooh girl, I am so through dealing with this knucklehead. I knew from the beginning that I did not need to get tied up with him. Him and his smooth talking self – walking around acting like the world revolves around him. What am I doing? This thing we are doing – it's just about sex – there is absolutely no relationship involved. He is so unreliable. I can't count on him to follow through with anything he says, yet, whenever he calls, I am right there like some love-sick fool, not to mention the fact that he has so much baggage. He is not mentally or emotionally in a place to love me the way I deserve to be loved. What was I thinking? When he gets back in town on Thursday, I am going to let him know. It's over. I am done. It's a wrap."

### Thursday night
(phone call from him):

"Hey Sunshine, how are you? I just got back in town from my business trip, and I could not stop thinking about you. You know I missed you and couldn't get back here quick enough. I know, I know – I've been tripping lately, but Tanya, you know there is no one as important to me as you are. I miss you so much when I am away. I can't wait to see you.

Can I come over?"

### Saturday afternoon
(lunch with girlfriend):

"Yeah girl, I know what I said, but ..."

---------------------------------

Does this sound familiar? Have you been there? You know what I am talking about – caught up in that cycle of destruction that we call love but in many instances is just another case of lust. We say that we are done and that we are not going back because we deserve more than just a sexual relationship. We get all pumped up and ready to lay down the law ... and then ... the phone rings ... and it's him ... in that oh-so-sexy voice that gets you every time. And even though you have rehearsed and rehearsed what you were going to tell him about himself, it all goes out the window right about the time that he tells you how much he has missed you. And then hours later, you find yourself wrapped right back up in his sheets ... **yet again**.

Or perhaps you are one of the people living in a fantasy world thinking that you can separate sex between a "physical" thing and an "emotional" thing, believing that there is something called "just sex" that won't have any impact or affect on you once you finish the act of sex. This is the mindset that a lot of men carry, and unfortunately enough, many women too. Some women feel like they can sleep with a person and not be emotionally tied to him. You may think it's "just sex," but believe me, you are emotionally tied because you have become one with that person – something that was designed for the confines of a marriage covenant. The scriptures are plain and clear-cut when they speak of the two becoming one.

**Genesis 2: 24** and **Matthew 19:5**, and **Mark 10:6**
Therefore a man shall leave his father and mother and be joined to his wife, and they shall become one flesh.

# FROM PROMISCUITY
## To Proverbs 31

Unfortunately, the principal of two becoming one stands no matter who that person is with whom you are intimate. I Corinthians 6:16 says, *Or do you not know that he who is joined to a harlot is one body with her? For 'the two' He says, "shall become one flesh.* Why do you think throughout scripture, whenever a man and woman had sex the Bible says, *They knew each other?* There is a level of internal knowledge that results from this level of intimacy. During sex, you allow your partner into your most sacred place, a place that was designed only for your spouse. It was never and is still not in God's plan for there to be a revolving door to that sacred place. The sexual union is designed by God to be a self-giving and mutually fulfilling bond that is extremely powerful – physically, emotionally and spiritually. It is powerfully releasing and unifying when expressed through God's plan for marriage, but it is also powerfully *destructive* when expressed outside of the marriage covenant. Yet, we feel like we can play with this "power" and not be affected by it. *Can one take fire into his or her bosom and not be burned?*

~~~~~~~~~~~~~~~~~~~~~~

**Proverbs 6:27-28**
Can a man take fire into his bosom, and his clothes not be burned?
Can one walk on hot coals and his feet not be seared?

~~~~~~~~~~~~~~~~~~~~~~

How is it that we can be so educated and know so much about world issues, politics, the industry in which we work, the latest fashion trends, etc., but have no clue when it comes to the issues of the heart? We allow just anyone to have access to our heart strings, and then we wonder why we keep getting "caught up." Unfortunately, over time we get "caught up" quicker and quicker. Remember when you were still a virgin? There was some level of standards that we considered. We were not going to let just anybody get too close too quickly. But once we had sex the first time, we let our guard down a little. If that relationship didn't work, the period between the beginning of the next dating relationship, and when we were intimate the first time was probably a little shorter than when we had sex the very first time. If *that* relationship didn't pan out, the time between the first hello and the sheets got even shorter the next go around. For some, the time got so short that it seemed like the first hello happened in somebody's sheets. Why is that? Simply stated ... we were (are) caught up in a cycle of destruction, and we become immune to values, boundaries, standards and morals.

Take a moment and examine yourself. Surely, you too can point out the cycle of destruction in your life as well. Most likely in the midst of finding the trail of the cycle, you can also pinpoint a trend because we tend to do the same thing and make the same dumb choices again and again. When I stopped and looked back over my years of dating, I definitely noticed a trend. For me, I often got involved with men who were not physically, emotionally and/or mentally "free" to date me. In other words – there was no "threat of commitment." It never reached the point to where I dated a married man, but had I not been delivered, it could have very well been my next move. Although they were not married, there was always something there – whether it was a job, their boys, or maybe even another woman on some level. And yet, somehow they managed to walk into my life (and my heart) and set up residence there. Now, had I known someone in the same predicament, I would have advised her to flee the scene. I can hear myself now, "Girlfriend, you are too good for that nonsense. You need to respect yourself if you expect him to respect you." Yet there I was in the midst of my own cycle of destruction because I could always come up with a justification for why "this time was different."

Isn't it funny how much easier it is to dish advice to someone else when we can't even take it for our own lives? Why is it so easy for us to point out when someone else is in an unhealthy relationship or acting foolish over a man or woman? Yet, when it's our own situation, we have on blinders. What is the plank in your eye? What "Godly" advice are you giving, but not applying to your own life? What sexual sin has you tied up in bondage because you have not admitted to yourself that it is sin?

---

**Matthew 7:1 -5**

[1] "Judge not, that you be not judged.

[2] For with the judgment you pronounce you will be judged, and the measure you give will be the measure you get.

[3] Why do you see the speck that is in your brother's eye, but do not notice the log that is in your own eye?

[4] Or how can you say to your brother, 'Let me take the speck out of your eye,' when there is the log in your own eye?

[5] You hypocrite, first take the log out of your own eye, and then you will see clearly to take the speck out of your brother's eye

---

Typically our cycles of destruction have a twist: there's often a flip side to the story. For me, the flip side of my story was not being able to recognize a good man. So whenever I met one, I grew tired easily and always found a reason why it wouldn't work. Was I begging for pain? Was I looking for heartbreak? No, but a part of me still didn't believe that I deserved a good man because I still hadn't forgiven myself for the things I had done in the past. Remember that man that I talked about in chapter 2 – *my sugar daddy?* Although he was gone from my life, the baggage that I took from the relationship was still haunting me. So instead of seeking whole, fulfilling relationships, I found myself in mere sexual relationships with the same man - just with a different name, height, weight, complexion and occupation. Yes, I was caught in a cycle of destruction. Are you caught there too? Are you struggling to break free from your sexual past? Are you tired of ending up in the same place time and time again – just with a different person? What steps do you need to take to finally break that cycle?

My cycle of destruction caused me to learn the hard way the strength of a sexual soul tie. The power that is released when a man and woman come together sexually is no joke. As we learned earlier, it is a connection that God clearly designed for a husband and wife to become as one; however, when we fornicate, we become joined to people who God did not intend for us to be yoked with because that power is still present. This is why, even when you come to your senses and realize that you are caught up with a knucklehead, you can't seem to get away. You have become *as one* with him or her, making it that much harder to break free.

Doctors and educators teach us that when you sleep with a person, you are in essence sleeping with everyone with whom they have slept. From a physical or health standpoint, you are opening yourself up to everything to which your partner has been exposed – but it's deeper than that. Spiritually, you are doing the same thing. You have now opened up your spirit man to be entangled by every yoke and spirit to which they have been exposed. You have become one with not only your partner, but also every spirit, stronghold and yoke that they are carrying. That's why it is imperative that you pray and ask God to destroy those soul ties in your life.

Over the years, I've talked to married people who did not take the time to break those ties, and now they don't understand why in the midst of making love to their husbands and wives, they are thinking of a past lover. It's unclear to them why now that they have a "license" to have sex, they have no desire. This unfortunate situation is because they have a whole line of past lovers in their bedroom with them and their spouse. No, they are not physically present, but they are spiritually and emotionally woven into their sexual experience. Their sacred place has been contaminated, and only God can clean it up.

Now, when I first discovered the cycle of destruction that was running my life, it wasn't even a spiritual matter for me - it was a common sense matter. I was just growing tired of selling myself short, settling for lust and calling it love. I was going to church regularly, but I was far from having a personal relationship with Christ. So when it came to His mandates, I was still treating the Bible like a smorgasbord – picking and choosing and contemplating what I was going to adhere to in my life. And at this point in time, not fornicating did not make the cut of rules by which I chose to abide. When I look back and think about that time in my life, it amazes me that I actually thought *that* was okay. My attitude towards God was, "I know you don't expect me to just stop doing everything. I gotta have some fun... it's just this one thing. I'm not hurting anyone." But in reality I was destroying myself.

You see, every time I entered into a sexual relationship, I was desensitizing myself and becoming numb to the conviction of fornication. Routine sin became the norm, and to stop seemed impossible. But this type of cycle is deadly because we reap what we sow.

### Galatians 6:7-8
We are not to be deceived, God is not mocked; for whatever a man sows, that he will also reap. For he who sows to his flesh will of the flesh reap corruption, but he who sows to the Spirit will of the Spirit reap everlasting life.

So tell me, what are you sowing? What will your harvest reap in your life? Don't be like me - so caught up that I didn't even have a desire to be free. As a matter of fact, I thought I was free – free to explore my sexuality that is. On the few occasions that I did actually pick up my Bible to read it outside of Sunday service, I was able to skip right over those scriptures that talked about fornicators and how they would not inherit the Kingdom of God. And if the pastor was speaking on fornication in service, I was able to tune that out too, as if it did not apply to me.

Grace and mercy became popular words in my vocabulary. I felt like I was covered because the Bible did say that we are all sinners and fall short of the glory of God ... so He expects us to mess up sometimes – so it's like we have a license to sin, right? **Absolutely NOT**. Romans 6:1-4 says, *What shall we say then? Shall we continue in sin that grace may abound? Certainly not! How shall we who died to sin live any longer in it? Or do you not know that as many of us as were baptized into Christ Jesus were baptized into His death? Therefore we were buried with Him through baptism into death, that just as Christ was raised from the dead by the glory of the Father, even so we should also walk in the newness of life.*

Are you in that place where I was ... realizing that I had to end this cycle, but feeling like that was an impossible task? Even as you are reading this book, a little voice may be trying to convince you that you are too far in to walk out of this lifestyle. You may be convinced that it is impossible, but Luke 18:27 tells us that *the things which are impossible with men are possible with God.* And then in Philippians 4:13, we are reminded that *we can do all things through Christ who strengthens us.* God is waiting for you to make the decision and to make that first step so that He can meet you there. Won't you step out? It won't be an easy step, but it is indeed a possible step. I am a living testimony that God will meet you right where you are. He will destroy every yoke, every stronghold. He is simply waiting on you to take the first step.

# CHAPTER 5: TWO FACES OF SALVATION
## From Freaky Fridays To Sunday Worship

# FROM PROMISCUITY
## To Proverbs 31

Let me ask you a question: how many times have you laid up in the arms of your lover who was **NOT** your spouse on a Sunday morning and invited him or her to church with you? And if you are anything like I was, then you probably became very indignant if he or she turned down the offer. *How dare you not be willing to serve my God?* Or how many times have you left Bible Study and went and spent the night with your boyfriend or girlfriend? How many times have you prayed with or studied the Word with your mate and turned right around and slept with him or her? Been there. Done that - until one day God asked me a question that threw me for a loop:

> **"Dear daughter, when are YOU going to start serving me by keeping my commands? When are you going to hang up the masks and stop switching roles from Super Saint to Super Freak? Pick a lane and stay in it. Either you will serve me or you will serve flesh. You simply cannot have it both ways. Choose one."**

Super Saint to Super Freak ... back to Super Saint again. Let me rewind this story a little and introduce you to my two faces of salvation, although you may already be acquainted since there are many of us who live double lives. You may just be one of them. In 1996, I re-dedicated my life to Christ and for a few months I was totally committed to obeying I Peter 1: 14-16, which states *as obedient children, not conforming yourselves to the former lusts, as in your ignorance; but as He who called you is holy, you also be holy in all your conduct, because it is written, Be holy, for I am holy.* So after I re-dedicated, I made some radical decisions and commitments for my life. I was 100% invested, and I was on my way to being "super-saint." So I thought ...

...That is until one day flesh rose up and reclaimed what it thought was its territory in my life. One moment, I was seemingly exercising self-control in this area and maintaining my commitment to abstinence, and the next moment – abstinence was no longer a part of my vocabulary. The spirit of sexual sin had attacked me and won. It wasn't a forceful attack – no, the enemy knows exactly what to do to entice us. He knew he couldn't bust back up in my life and demand that I return to my former ways. Instead, he eased his way back in through the back door I left open when I didn't spend the necessary time in prayer and studying my word.

### II Timothy 2:15
Study to show yourself approved, a worker who
does not need to be ashamed, rightly dividing the word of truth.

He set up traps as I continued to read my erotica novels that I thought were harmless. He slipped in by catching me without my armor and ammunition – you know, like when you thought you could still spend the night with your boyfriend, but maintain your new commitment to abstinence, even though it had only been 2 weeks since you made the commitment.

What about you? Have you left doors open for the enemy to come back (with all *his friends*) and set up residence? What is the trap that is being used in your life? Do you still regularly sleep over at your significant other's house? Do you still engage in sexual conversations? Do you play the "how far can we go" game? Or perhaps you call it the "we can touch, but not enter in" game. Do you still engage in pornography, masturbation or oral sex? It's time to clean house and LOCK the doors!

Don't be fooled. The enemy is watching you for an opportunity to reclaim territory. He is not going out without a fight. The enemy will try to be clever and outsmart you to get back in. For me, he got back in by sending a good looking "Christian" man who carried the same spirit of sexual perversion that I did. The enemy knew exactly what kind of man would turn my head, and he knew that I was aware of the dangers of dating an unsaved man – so he sent a Bible-toting, church-going, speaking-in-tongues brother my way. This man was gorgeous, and of course he said and did all the right things. We even prayed together. So you know that my nose was wide open.

Things were going very well. We were really enjoying each other, and there seemed to be a very strong connection between us. What I didn't understand at that time was that our spirits connected and drew us to each other. Let me clarify: not the Holy Spirit, but the spirit of sexual perversion that we were both carrying. And when those two spirits connected, it would not be long before we found ourselves in a compromising position. Yes, on the outside looking in, it appeared that we were living our lives for Christ; however, behind closed doors, we were serving the god of our flesh. We were indeed saved, but very much sexually active. If I am REALLY honest, I had more sex *after* I rededicated my life to Christ than I did before.

STOP THAT! Don't turn your nose up at me. And don't even *try* to act surprised! Look around you – many of your Christian family and friends are doing the same thing. Humph ...YOU may be doing the same thing. On Wednesday night and Sunday morning, you can catch us in service. Many of us are even active in ministry, but just don't ask where we were or what we were doing Friday night. Unfortunately, many of us live this double life convinced that we are totally sold out to Christ. Because we keep our sex lives hidden from our Christian friends who are actually committed to a Christian lifestyle, we may end up with two sets of circles in which to run.  One group is filled by those with whom you discuss Sunday service and what God is doing in your life – "Hallelujah, Praise the Lord!"  Then you have the set of friends with whom you talk about your latest sexual encounter: "Oh girl, let me tell you about this new position" ... And sometimes the two circles cross over because some of those "Christian" friends are living the same double life you are living.

So here you are proclaiming to be saved, sanctified, and filled with the Holy Spirit – yet you are really straddling the fence and thinking its okay.  Don't be fooled into this train of thought because the Bible is clear about being a lukewarm Christian – there is no middle ground and no room for compromise.  You must choose which God you will serve.  Revelation 3:15 says, *I know your works, that you are neither cold nor hot, I will vomit you out of my mouth.* God says that He will vomit us out of his mouth for trying to straddle the fence.

Webster's states:

To "vomit" is to be discharged forcefully and abundantly; spew or gush.

Do you really want God to discharge you forcefully from His Kingdom?  Do you want to be one of the ones who gets to heaven to hear Him say, *Not everyone who says to Me, 'Lord, Lord' shall enter the kingdom of God of heaven, but he who does the will of my Father in heaven.  Many will say to Me, Lord, Lord, have we not prophesied in Your name, cast out demons in Your name, and done wonders in Your name?"  And then I will declare to them, 'I never knew you; depart from Me, you who practice lawlessness!* (Matthew 7:21-23).

If you had to stand before God right now, would He receive you into His Kingdom?

What really amazes me about us lukewarm Christians is how easy it is to listen to the Word going forth and how quickly we grab hold of all the good stuff - you know, all of the scriptures that talk about all the blessings God wants to bestow upon us. I remember walking around declaring that I was blessed in the city and blessed in the country, blessed when I come in and when I go out ... until God reminded me that I was declaring His promises but that none of that mattered if I failed to adhere to His commands.

In Deuteronomy 28:1 it says, Now it shall come to pass, **IF YOU DILIGENTLY OBEY THE VOICE OF THE LORD YOUR GOD, TO OBSERVE CAREFULLY ALL HIS COMMANDMENTS ... then there comes a list of blessings you will receive.** But you don't get the part B (the blessings) without being obedient to part A (the commandments).

Then there were periods in my life (after salvation) that I really thought I had repented for my sexual sins and was ready to clean up my act which typically followed a pregnancy scare or a broken relationship. You know those times that you cry out to God with everything within you that you are sorry and will turn from your wicked ways. "Oh God, this is the last time! I promise!" Sound familiar? This became too familiar in my life. Asking for forgiveness became a routine. Have sex, ask for forgiveness, have sex again. They were just words coming out of my mouth.

Can you recall a similar situation in your life? Have you been there? Have you ever said, "God, please don't let me be pregnant. If you give me another chance – I will never disobey you again." So then the EPT comes back negative and what happens? A few weeks later, maybe even a few days later – you are right back in those sheets again. That, my dear, is not repentance. That is just you applying for a little "insurance."

**Repent** means to:

1. To feel remorse, contrition, or self-reproach for what one has done or failed to do; be contrite.
2. To feel such regret for past conduct as to **change** one's mind regarding it.
3. To make a **change** for the better as a result of remorse or contrition for one's sins.

True repentance requires a **change**. Without change, repentance does not take place. And don't try to justify your actions by thinking that it is better to forego repentance if you aren't ready to make that change because you are still held accountable for what you know. Hebrews 10:26 says, *for if we sin willfully after we have received the knowledge of the truth, there no longer remains a sacrifice for sins.*

**2 Peter 2:20-22**
For if, after they have escaped the pollutions
of the world through the knowledge of the
Lord and Savior Jesus Christ, they are again entangled
in them and overcome, the latter end is worse for them
than the beginning. For it would have been better for them
not to have known the way of righteousness, than having
known it, to turn from the holy commandment delivered
to them. But it has happened to them according to the true
proverb: "a dog returns to his own vomit and a sow having
washed, to her wallowing in the mire."

How many times will we say we are sorry and go right back to that same place? I will never forget the moment that changed my life. I had been abstinent for awhile and things occurred, and I found myself caught back up. One night, while lying in his arms, I did my routine cry out to God that I was sorry. At that moment, I caught this image of him nodding His head and throwing up his arms like, "Yeah, whatever." When it really hit me how disappointed God must have been, I was overwhelmed. When I repented that night, it wasn't just words – a **change** followed. True repentance had taken place, and my life would be forever impacted.

So tell me, what do your two faces of salvation look like? Are you singing praises unto God on the praise team on Sunday morning, yet singing praises unto your boyfriend or girlfriend in your bedroom Sunday night? How much longer do you think you can continue living these two lives before you are exposed? Are you ready for true repentance to take place in your life? Are you ready to be fully invested? He is still waiting ...

**II Chronicles 7:14**
If my people who are called by My name will humble
themselves, and pray and seek My face, and turn from
their wicked ways, then I will hear from heaven,
and will forgive their sin and heal their land.

# CHAPTER 6: FIGHTING FAMILIAR SPIRITS
*Change Of Mind Without A Change Of Heart*

If you were a recovering alcoholic, would you spend your free time in a bar? If you were a recovering drug addict, would you go hang out at the local crack house? No, of course not! Why not? Simply because the temptation to indulge in your previous addiction would be too strong, making it very easy to slip back into your old ways. Even the justice system knows how powerful strongholds are. For this reason, they don't allow convicted pedophiles to live within a certain distance of a school - fearing that the sight of the little kids will cause them to molest again.

Yet as Christians, we don't seem to have a problem returning to the things, the atmosphere, and the surroundings from which we continuously find ourselves praying for deliverance. We say that we want to abstain from sex, but we continue to spend the night with our significant other. We say we want to abstain from sex, yet we indulge in sexual conversations with our friends. We say that we want to abstain from sex, but we continue to plan candlelight dinners with Luther Vandross playing in the background and lingerie as our dinner attire. We say we want to abstain from sex, but we continue to read and watch pornographic material. We say that we want to abstain from sex, but we still go to the strip clubs to get a lap dance. We say we want to abstain from sex, but we never share that commitment to those closest to us. And then we are dumbfounded as to why we can't seem to **get out of that cycle of destruction.** We wonder why we have to keep asking for forgiveness for the same sin again and again. But how many times will we continue to cry out that *this is the last time*, Lord?

I remember clearly the day I stopped and asked myself that very question – how many more times would I promise God this was the last time? Then I took inventory. I looked closely at my habits and actions, and I looked at my inner circle. The words coming out of my mouth were "this is the last time," but there was no change in my routine. I was doing the same things that I was doing prior to making that declaration – so why in the world did I expect things to be different? I've often heard people define insanity as *doing the same thing over and over, but expecting a different result.* If this is the definition, it would be accurate to say that many of us are borderline insane.

So there I was, declaring that I was no longer going to defile my temple, that I was going to flee fornication and present my body a living sacrifice, holy and acceptable to God. Yes sir, yes ma'am – I was going to walk in victory in the area of sexual integrity. My past sexual sins were behind me, and I was pressing forward toward the mark of the high calling of Jesus Christ. Yes, I was preaching myself happy declaring every scripture I could think of and two hours later, I would be somewhere crying out to God that I was sorry for sleeping with my boyfriend yet again ... repenting for the same sin – over and over and over again. So I thought ...

The truth of the matter is that no repentance had taken place. Remember in order to repent, I had to turn from my sin. I had to change my mind regarding my past conduct. I had to make a change for the better as a result of remorse or contrition for my sins. That *is* what repentance means, right? So why did I think that I could sleep with him last night – get up the next morning, and cry out to the Lord that this was the last time, but then go spend the night at his house that same night and think, "He is just going to hold me tonight." You know what happened ... the next morning was like deja-vu as I cried out that I was sorry ... one more time. Where was the change? There wasn't one – it was all talk. I really *was* upset that I kept disappointing God, but not upset enough to "inconvenience" myself by making a change.

Plain and simple – a <u>change</u> has to take place. A <u>change</u> in your conversations. A <u>change</u> in your activities. A <u>change</u> in your choices. A <u>change</u> in your heart. Walking around just quoting scriptures won't get it. Even the devil knows the scripture! Change is an action word. So I ask you just as I had to ask myself, what changes do you need to make in your life? What routines need to be broken? What boundaries need to be set?

It is imperative that we don't just make up in our mind to abstain, but that we make a "heart" change. Webster defines the heart as:

    a. The vital center and source of one's being, emotions, and sensibilities.
    b. The repository of one's deepest and sincerest feelings and beliefs.
    c. The seat of the intellect or imagination.

The heart is the seat of our emotions, and we all know that when our heart is all over the place – so are we. We must guard our hearts and not allow everything and everybody to have full access to it. We have to watch what enters into our heart because it is delicate. It is our driving force and must be handled with care.

A very familiar scripture that is often quoted about the heart is Proverbs 4:23. It says that we *must keep our heart with all diligence, for out of it spring the issues of life.* Matthew 12:34b goes on to say *for out of the abundance of the heart the mouth speaks.*

## To Keep:

1. To retain possession of
2. To maintain for use or service
3. To manage, tend, or have charge of
4. To preserve
5. To cause to continue in a state, condition, or course of action

6. To adhere or conform to
7. To be faithful to; fulfill

### Dil·i·gence:

1. Earnest and persistent application to an undertaking; steady effort; assiduity.
2. Attentive care; heedfulness.

According to Webster's dictionary, "to keep" is to *retain possession of, to manage, to have charge of.* "Diligence" means *attentive care; earnest and persistent application to an undertaking.* So when the scripture tells us to guard our hearts with all diligence, we cannot regard it as a fly-by-night command. It takes real action to keep your heart with all diligence. It means that you will have to make some unpopular decisions sometimes. It may come down to you not listening to everything that everyone else is listening to, and not watching everything that everyone else is watching. You definitely can't go everywhere that everyone else is going.

Throughout scripture, God reveals how important the heart is. The scriptures show us how every thought and action stem from the position of our heart. It's simple: what you put in is what you get out.

### Proverbs 2:10-16

*When wisdom enters your heart, and knowledge is pleasant to your soul, discretion will preserve you; understanding will keep you, to deliver you from the way of evil, from the man who speaks perverse things, from those who leave the paths of uprightness to walk in the ways of darkness; who rejoice in doing evil, and*

*delight in the perversity of the wicked; whose ways
are crooked, and who are devious in their paths;
(Men, verse 16 is for you) To deliver you from
the immoral woman, from the seductress
who flatters with her words.*

### Proverbs 23:7
*For as he thinks in his heart, so is he.*

### Luke 6:45
*A good man out of the good treasure of his heart
brings forth good; and an evil man out of the evil
treasure of his heart brings forth evil. For out of the
abundance of the heart his mouth speaks.*

### Matthew 15:18-19
*But those things which proceed out of the
mouth come from the heart, and they defile
a man. For out of the heart proceed evil
thoughts, murderers, adulteries, fornications,
thefts, false witnesses and blasphemies.*

### Proverbs 27:19
*As in water face reflects face, so a man's heart reveals the man.*

---

The last scripture – Proverbs 27:19, says *as in water face reflects face, so a man's heart reveals the man.* What is your heart revealing about you? Think about it. If you were to look into a body of water, you would see a reflection of you – an identical reflection. It's not a magic mirror that will show you just what you want to see. It's going to show you what is actually there. It is the same with our hearts. We can pretend to be whatever we want to be, but whatever is in our hearts will be revealed through both our words and our actions. So again I ask you, what is your heart revealing about you? Just how committed are you to really abstaining until marriage? What are you doing to assure you maintain that commitment? Have you been diligently keeping your heart and what enters into it or barely guarding it?

Like I said before, when I began to ask myself that question, I looked around and realized that I might as well have been running through a land mine, just waiting for an explosion because I was still living a life suited for my past, sexually immoral lifestyle - not my present commitment to abstinence. I was still entertaining sexually stimulating conversations, staying the night at my boyfriends regularly, still on birth control pills, and R. Kelly's "I Don't See Nothing Wrong With A Little Bump And Grind" was still in rotation in my cd player. Do you see where I am going here? Nothing had changed in my life to prepare or equip me to walk in sexual integrity. Yet I expected a miraculous change.

It's also important to note that many of my hanging out buddies did not even *know* about my new commitment, and many of them honestly just wouldn't have understood anyway. When I really decided to change, I quickly learned how important it was to have people around who would hold me accountable. Just as I had to reevaluate my friendships, you need to take inventory of those in your inner circle. It doesn't help you to be disciplined if everyone with whom you are walking is still having sex. During one of my first attempts at abstinence, I called up one of my girlfriends because the temptation was getting too much for me to handle. I called her and told her that my boyfriend was in the shower and had invited me to join him. Her response was, "Why are you on the phone with me? You better go join him." Talk about no accountability whatsoever! What happened to reminding me of the commitment I had made to abstinence? Or reminding me of what the Word says about fornication. Now perhaps you are thinking this was a sister who was not saved, but actually, she was a sister from my college ministry – a very active sister in the ministry at that. I guess she was still suffering from that smorgasbord mentality of picking and choosing which commandments to follow. I cannot stress enough how imperative it is that you surround yourself with people who share your same commitments. Does your inner circle consist of people who will hold you accountable for your decisions or ones who will give you an excuse to sin? What things, people or activities in your life are suited for your past sins and not your present commitments?

**Proverbs 12:26**
The righteous should choose his friends carefully,
for the way of the wicked leads them astray.

**Proverbs 13:20**
He who walks with wise men will be wise, but the
companion of fools will be destroyed.

**Proverbs 27:17**
As iron sharpens iron, so a man sharpens the
countenance of his friend.

This journey of abstinence 'til marriage can get lonely sometimes, especially when you begin to say "no" to some of the things and even the people from your past. The journey can even be discouraging at times, making you want to throw in the towel and return to your former ways; but speaking from experience, there is no freedom like the freedom found in letting go of your sexual sins.

When you begin to treat your body as the temple that God created it to be, there is a place of oneness with God that you can never obtain while indulging in sexual sin. Turn that passion that drives you towards sex into passion that will drive you to worship God – and watch how your intimate relationship with God develops to levels of which you've never dreamed. As you continue to draw into Him, you will find yourself further and further away from your past cycle of sexual sin.

## CHAPTER 7: DIVORCING SIN
### When Enough Is Finally Enough

What happens once you accept that you are stuck in a cycle of destruction and living two lives? What happens when you are ready to really commit to a life of abstinence until marriage? What happens when you have done everything you can think of to make a change in your life and realize that this is something only God can do? What happens when you have cried out "I am sorry" for the last time, yet you are still lying in some man or some woman's arms? What happens when you are tired of dishing out parts of yourself to people across the nation who are not your spouse? What happens when you finally look in the mirror and say, "This is not the life that God intended for me!"? This point is where you take a step away from your sinful ways and take a step towards God, and He will meet you right there. This is where your journey to deliverance will begin.

---

**I John 1:9**
If we confess our sins, He is faithful and just to forgive us our sins and to cleanse us from all unrighteousness.

**James 4:8a**
Draw near to God and He will draw near to you.

---

Over the course of time, I made several unsuccessful attempts to live a life of abstinence before I had a successful attempt. Many times the attempts failed simply because I had not really made up in my heart that I was going to change. I was just weeping about my sin until the opportunity presented itself again. I was going through the motions of repentance, but I was really just hoping my sin wouldn't catch up with me. I was saying, "I'm sorry God"

because I knew it was the "right" thing to do, but I knew that night I would be wrapped right back up in those sheets again. As a matter of fact, early on I was looking forward to being back there. Do you know what I am talking about? You know, when we promise God if we get off the hook this time we will NEVER do this again. Right ... how many of those promises have we broken?

However, once you truly give your heart to God and the more time you spend in His word and in His presence, being in sin is no longer a comfortable place. Sin will lose all of its flavor, excitement and fun. You may even find yourself doing some things out of mere habit and not because it's what you want to do. Near the end of my journey of sexual sin, it still "felt" good. Yes, I still enjoyed it in that moment, but the conviction that would set in afterwards and sometimes during was getting so strong that I started to think to myself, "Is it really worth all of this?" I had grown tired of the tears and tired of disappointing myself and God, and I was ready to make a change in my life. It was at that moment that my first sincere repentance took place.

When I was really ready to "walk out" this thing called abstinence, I was in search of information on how to be successful at it. Where do I start? Is there an 8-step plan to get rid of this addiction? I was searching and searching hard. I began to go to Abstinence seminars and workshops. I always felt like the lady in the movie, *The Scarlet Letter*. I would sit there soaking in all the information about why it was important to wait until marriage to have sex. I sat there as they encouraged the attendees to not "unwrap" the gift until they were married, to cherish their virginity, to save themselves. I would begin to condemn myself because my gift had been unwrapped, rewrapped and unwrapped several more times. Often at that very moment of condemnation, there would be a plug for those of us who were not virgins. It went something like, "And if you aren't a virgin – it's not too late ...." Ok God, that's great, but how do I walk this thing out?

A part of me thought that it would be an instantaneous thing. I would make the commitment and POOF, there would no longer be a struggle. Of course that did not happen. So there I was in a struggle, not knowing how to get out. Along the way, I failed a few times, and in the beginning when I failed I was very hard on myself. Often times, I even thought about just throwing in the towel because obviously this was an impossible task. It didn't take long for me to realize that it was not as easy as just saying, "I am not going to do this anymore," but it did start with making the decision. Simply put, you have a choice to follow God's command to avoid sexual immorality or to continue walking in sexual sin. Just make a decision. I did. Will you?

*But what's next?* I kept asking myself. And you are probably asking yourself the same question. What do I do, and is there anyone that I can talk to? The people who knew I was sexually active were not in a position to teach me how to abstain because they were having sex too. And I was too embarrassed to talk to the people who could have walked with me because they were living a life of abstinence. There was no way I was going to let them into my secret closet of my past sexual sins. So I fumbled through on my own looking for answers and quick fixes, but we all know there is no such thing as a quick fix. I quickly discovered that I didn't have the answers, and because of that I made many mistakes along the journey - BUT GOD.

My first mistake was substituting suppression for deliverance. I tried to skip "the process" of deliverance by completely avoiding any situation that would result in a possible struggle. That might sound like a good plan, but that's where I got hung up. In an effort to avoid sexual activity, I began to spend time and date people where there was no sexual attraction to begin with (and would never be). So here I am feeling good that I was staying out of trouble when the truth of the matter was I wouldn't have slept with these guys even if I wasn't trying to abstain. It didn't take any effort to say "no" when I wasn't interested anyway. I wasn't dealing with my problem; I was just running from it. And the first time a tall, sexy chocolate appeared on the scene – Lord, have mercy - I realized just how hard this walk was really going to be.

However, one of the first smart things I started to do when I got serious about my commitment was to become very vocal about my decision. I shared my stance on first dates. That may seem extreme, but there was no point in having a 2nd date with a guy who didn't respect my commitment - or better yet, if we didn't have the same commitment. This also eliminated a lot of future heartaches and headaches. It blew my mind sometimes the responses I received like, "Well, I haven't made that decision, so perhaps we can come up with a compromise." Or "Wait, let me make sure I got this right – you are abstaining just until you are in a committed relationship, not until marriage, right?" Or the best one, "Oh, you may have been abstaining up until now, but you won't be able to resist me." That day, I wish the scripture had said, "Slap the fool – and then flee fornication!"

In talking about abstinence early, I still had to discern motives because people know how to say all the right things; but just like it's a challenge to break in a virgin (to be their first sexual encounter), there is a sense of challenge to convince someone to go against their decision to abstain. You know how it is anytime you are told that you can't have something you want – it makes you want it more. So while their mouths were saying, "I understand, I accept that," their minds were already plotting a trap for me, strategizing on how to get me in bed regardless of my decision.

Being real, especially with myself, was also very important. I started talking to other people who had been abstaining for YEARS and at first, they were all giving me these super holy answers pretending like they were never tempted. At that time, I was sitting there thinking I must just be a sex addict because this is definitely not an easy walk for me, so what the heck are they talking about? Those feelings don't just go away, and you don't want them to go away – you just want to be able to control them.

Finally, I came across a woman who kept it real with me and admitted that she had to crucify her flesh daily to be successful in her stance. She was very transparent about her close calls and her *almost mishaps,* and the one thing she told me was to never act like there was no struggle. She made sure I realized that there was no formula for abstinence. She told me never to get big-headed and so confident in myself that I thought it was impossible to slip up. Her biggest plea was for me to never pretend to always have it together, especially when a recent committer turned to me for help with his or her journey. She said, "They need to know that it's not always a cake walk." Her words and example stuck with me, which is one of the many reasons why when people ask about my commitment I always keep it real. I am open to share the good, the bad and the ugly of my journey thus far.

Although I was equipped with her wise advice, I still failed. In the beginning of the book, I shared a journal entry which was written one week before my two year anniversary of being abstinent. Are you wondering what happened? How did I fall? At some point on my journey, I did what she had told me not to do, and I got big-headed. I forgot that it was God who had given me the strength to make it for almost two years. Like many before me, I began to put the confidence in my own abilities instead of God's grace. I got a little cocky thinking that I simply could not fall. You know, according to me, "I got this thing under wraps – it's all good."

So I started "entertaining" sexual conversations with this guy to whom I was very much sexually attracted. I thought it was all innocent and that it was just talk because I thought I was in control. Unfortunately, that *talk* created an atmosphere of compromise for me to let down all my guards. And slowly but surely, I began to stretch past my set boundaries a little more every time I saw or talked to him. I had to learn the hard way that we have to watch our conversations if we are serious about living a holy life before God. Learn from my mistake; don't make your own in this area. Don't allow your thoughts or your words to misrepresent the life you are committed to living. Don't ever think, "It's just a conversation." Every word spoken is a seed sown, and you may not be equipped to handle the harvest when it springs forth – full grown.

### James 3:3-6
Indeed, we put bits in horses' mouths that they
may obey us, and we turn their whole body. Look
also at ships: although they are so large and are
driven by fierce winds, they are turned by a very
small rudder wherever the pilot desires. Even so the
tongue is a little member and boasts great things.
See how great a forest a little fire kindles! And the
tongue is a fire, a world of iniquity. The tongue is
so set among our members that it defiles the whole
body, and sets on fire the course of nature; and it
is set on fire by hell.

During my many conversations with this particular man - never, not even once did I even consider telling him I was committed to abstinence. By the tone and nature of our conversations, he never would have guessed it. Eventually, he said all the right things and did all the right things to get exactly what he wanted. And for that moment, I wanted it too, but afterwards, as I lay in his arms, I caught a glimpse of God looking at me shaking his head in disgust - **that was my breaking moment.** I knew then that the next man I was with would be my husband.

The decision was made, and I was ready to be 150% committed. I pictured myself walking in victory from sexual sins, and I was going to be able to bury my past...so I thought. When I first got serious about my commitment, I remember praying to God all excited that I was able to make this decision before all my actions were brought to the public eye. I had maintained my "innocent" image to those around me so no one ever had to know the life that I had lived behind close doors. My life was free of ever being on blast for my sexual sins. I was grateful that I had never gotten pregnant or gotten a Sexually Transmitted Disease (STD), etc ... but God had a different plan...

**Isaiah 55:8**
For my thoughts are not your thoughts,
Nor are your ways my ways says the Lord.

God said, "Share your story."

I said – "HA, are you serious! God did you hear what I just said about never having to lose my 'innocent' image?"

God said, "This is not about you. I am going to use you to minister to others with the same struggle and to bring me glory."

So as many do, I began my, "I am not qualified for this" speech - a speech that lasted for weeks, even months because I was convinced that the devil was trying to set me up.

"But God, who am I - the one barely out the sheets - to tell someone else that they should be committed to abstinence?"

Then one Wednesday night at church, this lady whom I had

never seen or talked to walked up to me during Pass The Peace (a part of my church's worship service where you greet your neighbor with a hug) and whispered in my ear, **"God said that you are qualified."** It was pretty much a wrap from there ...

And all of that has led me to where I am today - sharing my story with you. I am free to show you my scars so that you don't have to bear the same ones. If you are still reading this book, then I believe that you are in the place that I found myself in a few years ago - tired of abusing myself, tired of disappointing God, tired of sharing myself with men who were not my husband, tired of giving away a gift that was intended for only one man, tired of short changing myself...just tired.

I shared my struggle with you; now allow me to share the journey to victory in the same area. If I can be delivered, so can you! God is waiting for you to trust him. Will you do it? Will you reach out and grab His hand that He has always had extended to you? Won't you allow Him to teach you how to walk as the Righteousness of God? Won't you allow Him to cleanse you of all unrighteousness, to blot out all of your transgressions that you may be presented as a vessel of honor? Won't you listen as He whispers in your ear that you are the apple of His eye – His precious one? Won't you allow Him to embrace you? Come on ... I believe in you ... Take that first step ... Come, let's travel the journey to victory together ...

# PRAYER OF REPENTANCE

Father God, I come before you sincerely asking that you forgive me of my sins and wash all impurity from me. Lord, destroy this yoke of bondage that has a hold on me right now. Help me to take a stand and declare my body the living sacrifice that you so ordained for it to be.

Teach me, Father, who I am in you. Teach me, Father, what you designed sex for so that I will no longer pervert it. Lord, surround me with people who will hold me accountable to the standard of purity which you desire me to commit. Lord, destroy every memory that tries to creep back into my thoughts to draw me back. Break every soul tie. Destroy the covenants that I made with every man or woman with whom I have laid.

Renew my mind, renew my spirit – wash me whiter than snow. Lord, I desire to be a vessel of purity. So, as I walk through this process, teach me to be transparent that I may reach back and draw out others who find themselves stuck in this same place.

No longer will I allow the guilt and shame of my past to dictate my future. Yes, I did everything they said I did – but I know that is not who I am. Thank you Father for your continued grace and mercy. I will no longer take it for granted, nor will I abuse it.

I love you and commit on this day, _____(insert date)_____, that I will abstain from all levels of sexual impurity. I thank you for restoring my gift that I may present it to the mate you have created for me on the night of our marriage. I honor and glorify you, in Jesus' name. Amen.

# PART II

## THE VICTORY

# FROM PROMISCUITY
## To Proverbs 31

### Introduction: The Surgical Process

So you have decided to leave your life of sexual sin behind you and to walk as the righteousness of God. The question now becomes *how do you let go of the past and not allow it to mold your present?* I've said it over and over again: Your life in sexual sin developed over time, and your journey to victory in the same area will also take some time. Most of us dread the idea of "process"; however, it is very important, so go ahead and prepare yourself for the path before you. Don't be discouraged when the journey seems too tough to endure. Continue to remind yourself that you are not in this place alone. God is with you every step of the way. Don't search for quick remedies that will just coat the problem. We want to remove the roots which will take God's divine power and healing. At times this process may even feel like surgery - open heart surgery, maybe even triple by-pass surgery. The phases of this type spiritual surgery mirror a similar procedure in the natural, inclusive of pre-op procedures, ICU and post-op instructions. So brace yourself. The task won't be easy but it will be well worth the struggle.

### Pre-Op

People don't typically just wake up one day and decide they need surgery. The revelation comes after realizing that something is not right and can only be corrected through surgery. Often tests are done to accurately determine the root of the problem. The fact that you are still reading this book leads me to believe that you realize that you have a problem that needs divine healing. I believe that you are ready to commit to a life of abstinence until marriage.

Before surgery, the doctor always gives some pre-operation instructions because there is a preparation period prior to surgery.

Depending on the severity of the problem, the pre-op instructions could be a simple change in diet, while for others there may be a need for more in-depth changes. Regardless of what the instructions call for, they must be followed in order for the surgery to run smoothly. In this chapter, there will be some pre-op instructions, but you must remain open to the leading of the Holy Spirit because your surgery may require more. His guidelines for you may not always make sense, and you may think you have a better method, but remember that God always knows best.

### Proverbs 3:5-6
*Trust in the Lord with all your heart, and lean not on your own understanding. In all your ways acknowledge Him and He shall direct your path.*

## Intensive Care Unit

Due to the delicacy of the surgery, you will have to enter the ICU – Intensive Care Unit. Please be patient because you may have to stay awhile. Most of us need to shed many layers of sin residue, such as unforgiveness, guilt, shame, low self esteem, pain, soul ties, disappointment, and the list goes on and on. It's a delicate procedure which can even be painful, but it's necessary in order to rid yourself of the "sin buildup" in your life. During and after surgery, you will be placed in a very clean and sterile environment to help remove and keep out contaminates. Not everyone will be allowed into the ICU to visit with you, so don't get upset if you start feeling alone during the process. You will probably experience a range of emotions during surgery which is okay. Just let it all out and allow God to touch and cleanse your innermost parts. God wants to destroy the yokes and the strongholds and to remove all heaviness from your spirit so that you can move forward from this place.

---

### Psalm 30:5b

*Weeping may endure for a night, but joy comes in the morning.*

### Psalm 30:11-12

*You have turned for me my mourning into dancing.
You have put off my sackcloth and clothed me with
gladness. To the end that my glory (soul) may sing
praise to you and not be silent. O Lord my God, I
will give thanks to you forever.*

---

## Post-Op

Once you come out of surgery, post-op is just as critical. This time of healing is as important as the surgery itself. Contrary to popular opinion, you need a divine healing from God. You don't need a night at the club, a bottle of wine, a good girl talk, or a night out with the boys - you need God and His healing power. During post-op, you will be monitored carefully because those who hold you accountable need to make sure all traces of sexual sin have been removed.

Change is inevitable after surgery. There are some things that you do, places you go, people with whom you hang out, as well as things you watch and read, that don't line up with the changes that have been made internally. If you continue walking down the path that you were on prior to surgery, you will eventually end up in the same place. So be prepared for change as your heart and mind line up with your new commitment.

After surgery, you must eat the Word daily in order to feed your spirit instead of your flesh. You must study and embrace God's mandates and learn His principles regarding your body and your sexuality. You were "good" at being a sinner, and now it's time to be "good" at living right. You are a new man/woman, so it's time to walk in the image of God. Come out of the darkness and into the marvelous light!

---

### Ephesians 5:8
*For you were once darkness, but now you are light in the Lord. Walk as children of light.*

### Psalm 119:11
*Your word I have hidden in my heart, that I might not sin against you.*

---

# CHAPTER 8: THE PRE-OP PROCEDURES

Before your "surgery" begins, there are just a few things that need to be addressed to make sure you are properly prepared for the ICU process. You want to make sure you are able to fully embrace the transformation that will take place there, so don't try to skip out on the preparation period. Remember: It is just as important as the ICU process itself.

## FORGIVENESS FIRST

Have you ever been in a relationship and something happened that resulted in you causing the other party hurt and pain? You apologize, and though they are hurting, they say that they accept your apology. You all try to move on from that place of pain, but then every time you turn around they are reminding you about "the time you hurt them." Or perhaps they just act differently towards you because their mouth said they forgave you, but their heart just hadn't grabbed hold of the forgiveness yet. So you find yourself in this constant battle to prove that you are really sorry.

Fortunately for us, we serve a forgiving and gracious God who really means it when He forgives us. He isn't keeping score, and He won't keep throwing your past sin back in your face. Even when we don't deserve His forgiveness, He forgives us. So you can rest assured that when you finally come to the place of true repentance and tell God that you are sorry and want to walk away from a lifestyle of sexually immorality that He will really forgive you. John 1:9 says *if we confess our sins, He is faithful and just to forgive us our sins and to cleanse us from all unrighteousness.*

The problem typically arises in that we don't take the time to forgive ourselves, part of which comes from not believing that we are really forgiven. God isn't condemning us, but we continue to put ourselves in a state of condemnation which gives the enemy leverage in our lives. Although God doesn't throw our past up in our face, the devil will. Every chance he gets, he will remind us of our past sins and try to convince us that we are worthless, dirty, and full of sin. We have to remember that his assignment is to steal, kill and destroy. He wants to steal your joy, kill your spirit, and destroy your self-worth. The longer you walk around tripping on yourself because of your past sins and not accepting the redemption that you have in God, the longer you expose yourself to his attacks.

Other times, it's not even the devil throwing things in our face - it's us. We beat ourselves up by dwelling on the past. We become our own worst enemy, constantly reminding ourselves of who we once were. We remain in bondage to our sexual sins simply because we can't forgive ourselves. God forgave us and set us free, yet we can't walk in that freedom. By not forgiving ourselves, we become like a prisoner being released from jail, but who doesn't move from his jail cell because he keeps rehearsing his crime in his head. The jail cell door is wide open, and he has been issued his release papers, but he just stays there stuck because he can't forgive himself.

Sounds silly, right? But we do it to ourselves all the time. Forgiveness means *to pardon, to spare someone of the burden of their offense.* So when God has forgiven you, you no longer have to walk around carrying the burden or weight of your sin. Jesus took our sins upon Himself when he died on the cross, which made it possible for God to forgive us. We try to look at God's forgiveness the way humans forgive, but God's ability to forgive is much greater than ours. Psalms 103:12 says, *As far as the east is from the west, so far has He (God) removed our transgressions from us.* Hello my friend - that means infinite forgiveness. When God says, "Son or daughter, I forgive you", it's a done deal. No one can take that forgiveness away from you, so accept God's forgiveness and then forgive yourself. LET IT GO. You can't change the past, but you can keep the past from dictating your future. Until you are able to fully embrace God's forgiveness and forgive yourself, you won't be able to move forward in this process.

## DEAL WITH THE DISAPPOINTMENT

Have you ever longed for something to the point that the desire resonated from your heart and soul? Have you ever expected so much from a person that when they didn't come through, you felt the pain in your innermost parts? Have you ever set a goal for yourself and when you didn't attain the goal, it almost wiped away all the confidence you had in yourself? Have your parents or someone you were fond ever told you that you had disappointed them? Or even worse, have they ever disappointed you? Do you remember how it made you feel? Do you remember the void that began to form in your heart? Do you remember the iron gate walls that you subconsciously began to build to insure that no one else would ever have the opportunity to disappoint you again?

We have all been disappointed at some point in our lives especially in relationships; however, we cannot allow that feeling to control our lives. It can be very hard to cope with feelings of disappointment. This emotion can lead to feelings of distrust, betrayal, bitterness, and even hatred. Why does disappointment hurt so badly? Webster defines **disappointment** as *the failure to satisfy the hope, desire of expectation of or thwarted* (to oppose and defeat the efforts, plans or ambitions of) *in hope, desire or expectation.* To **hope** is *to wish for something with expectation of its fulfillment or to have confidence or trust in.* **Desire** is *to wish or long for or to want.* **Expectation** is *eager anticipation.* When our heart is set on something happening or someone coming through and that something falls through the crack, or that person doesn't keep his or her word, disappointment is birthed – and it hurts.

Think about how you felt the last time you were disappointed. How did you feel? How did you react or respond? How did it affect the way you treated the one who disappointed you?

But wait! Now think about how often we disappoint God. We continuously make promises that we don't keep. We continuously break his commandments and mandates. We continuously shrug off His attempts to lead us down a path of righteousness. We continuously misuse and abuse his unconditional love, yet He never turns his back on us. Even when we fail to say "I'm sorry," He's faithful to forgive us. Even when we fail to admit our wrongdoing, He keeps His word. Even when we pretend that it doesn't even matter, He still loves us.

Yet, when someone disappoints us, we can't handle it. We shut down or shut them out. When will we learn to show compassion, forgiveness and love in spite of how we feel? When will we learn to follow the standards that Christ set for us? If our eternal hope is placed in God who will never fail us, and if we begin to walk in love towards everyone including our enemies, disappointment won't have the power in our lives that it has now. If we can only begin to understand that people and things will let us down, we will be better able to bounce back from disappointments with our joy intact. Then one day, just like God, we will be able to continue to extend our hands and our hearts to those who disappoint us, but realizing that our minor disappointments can't even measure up to a percentage of the disappointment we cause God daily.

## FACE THE FACTS

One of the hardest challenges in life can be looking at ourselves for who and what we really are. All of us want to believe that we have it all together and have no faults, so when someone points out a fault in us, we flip out and lose it. However, if we could just face the facts about ourselves, people wouldn't be able to use our "areas of improvement" as leverage against us. The same is true with your past sexual immorality. You can't change what you did in the past, so you need to look your past in the eye and admit where you've been, what you've done, and even how it affected you. Face it, repent, accept God's forgiveness, forgive yourself and move forward.

Facing the facts about your past becomes ammunition in the future. You don't have to walk around worried about skeletons in your closet. You don't have to fear someone "exposing" you and your secrets because *you* have already brought it to light. You've already dealt with who you once were; therefore, no one can use your past against you. Now, when someone tries to remind you of your past, instead of running and wanting to crawl under a rock, you may even be able to use your past to minister to their present situation. You have to become comfortable with the place from where God has brought you. Baby, your past is the foundation for your praise report! I tell people all the time that if God could deliver me, I know He can deliver you.

Over the years, there are many things that I have done of which I was ashamed, but I had to face those things because the shame had me in bondage long after I had stopped committing sexual sins. I was always afraid of what someone might think if they knew that I had done this or done that, but none of that matters anymore. I jump at the opportunity to show and share my scars, especially if it will help keep the next person from making some of the bad decisions that I made. There was a time that I tried to justify everything I had done, blame it on someone else, or even sugar coat it. And for what? Those were all temporary solutions. It wasn't until I admitted my past, just like Isaiah proclaimed, *"Woe is me, for I am undone!"* that I was able to move forward.

Sexual addiction is just like any other addiction. The first step of deliverance for an alcoholic or a drug addict is admitting that they have a problem. Proverbs 28:13 says, *He who covers his sin will not prosper, but whoever confesses and forsakes them will have mercy.* Do you understand that you cannot truly repent of your sins until you face the facts and admit that you are in sin? You will never walk away from pornography, fornication, or masturbation until you admit that you are struggling in those areas. When you continue to pretend that there is not a struggle, you are simply lying to yourself and delaying your deliverance. Do you think that by not acknowledging your sin that you have God fooled? Psalm 69:5 says, *O God, you know my foolishness, and my sins are not hidden from you.* God knows everything there is to know about you. Allow Him to show you the *real* you. As you seek God, you will begin to see yourself in a true light. When this happens, acknowledge the sin in your life, repent and turn from that place, and move forward. You have tried to run from the truth for too long. Your time is here – simply **Face the Facts.**

## DECIDE WHO'S DADDY

Romans 6:18 says, *And having been set free from sin, you have become slaves of righteousness.* Before you repented of your sins, you were a slave to your sexual sin. That slavery is why you felt like you were in bondage, defeated by this stronghold. With God's forgiveness comes deliverance from your old master. So why do you still listen to your old master? If you have a new master, why are you still allowing your old master to tell you what to do? If you used to work at UPS and then switched teams to go work at FedEx, would you still accept orders from UPS? Would you allow your old supervisor at UPS to tell you what time to be at work, what time to leave, when to go on vacation? Absolutely not. So why is it that you repent of your sins, and commit to serving God, yet allow the devil to continue controlling your thoughts and actions? You don't have to listen to his lies anymore. His conversation is not even worth listening to, but you have to make a decision of who it is that you are going to serve. Who is your daddy now? *No servant can serve two masters; for either he will hate the one and love the other, or else he will be loyal to one and despise the other* (Luke 16:13a).

It's easy to get used to a familiar place, even if it's a place in which we no longer desire to be. We are just there because it's where we have been for so long, but you don't have to stay there any longer. Stop doing what you have always done. It's time to learn the rules for your new place, like getting a new job and going through new hire orientation and training. The company equips you with a handbook that tells you what it expects of you and what you can expect in return. When you decide to live your life for Christ, it's the same scenario. You get a handbook (The Bible) that is full of instructions and outlines what is expected of you. It also lets you know all of the benefits of fulfilling your end of the deal. It's critical that you stand strong in your new commitment because you will have many opportunities to break the commitment. So if you are shaky and wavering with your commitment, a fall is probably right around the corner for you – so you must be steadfast.

Ok, you've decided that you are going to serve God. So as instructed in Colossians 3:9-10 – *It's time to put off the old man with his deeds, and put on the new man who is renewed in knowledge according to the image of Him who created him.* Your actions have to line up with the master you are serving. When you were living for the devil (flesh), *you set your mind on things on the earth – fornication, uncleanness, passion, evil desire and covetousness* (Colossians 3:2-5). But now that *you are the elect of God, holy and beloved – you must set your mind on things above and put on tender mercies, kindness, humility, meekness, longsuffering and love* (Colossians 3: 12-14).

There should be evidence in your life that confirms which master you are serving. We already know that we cannot straddle the fence and that we have to choose one. You can try and pretend that you are serving God while feeding flesh, but the fruit you produce will tell all. You reap what you sow. What are you sowing? If you are still serving the devil (your flesh), you will continue to reap *adultery, fornication, uncleanness, lewdness, idolatry, sorcery, hatred, contentions, jealousies, outburst of wrath, selfish ambitions, dissensions, heresies, envy, murders, drunkenness, revelries and the like.* However, once you decide that God is your daddy, your fruit should *be love, joy, peace, longsuffering, kindness, goodness, faithfulness, gentleness and as it relates especially to sexual sins - SELF CONTROL!* So again I ask, who's your daddy?

## GET DRESSED FOR BATTLE

Throughout the scriptures, we are assured of the victory before even engaging in battle. Romans 8:31 states *that if God be for us, who can be against us.* And in verse 37, we are reminded that *we are more than conquerors through Christ Jesus.* Then Matthew 16:19 tells us that *we have been given the keys of the kingdom of heaven, and whatever we bind on earth will be bound in heaven, and whatever we loose on earth will be loosed in heaven.* Yes, we have the victory, but that does not give us permission to be nonchalant in battle.

In Ephesians 6, we are encouraged *to put on the whole armor of God that we may be able to stand against the wiles of the devil.* We must not ever get so confident that we forget that our strength comes from God and not ourselves. The enemy is always looking for a door, a window, even a small crack to enter and wreak havoc in our lives. You will never catch a soldier entering a battle without his armor, so why should we be any different? The scriptures paint a clear picture of the armor that we need in order to fight this spiritual battle. The six pieces are: *belt of truth, breastplate of righteousness, feet shod with the preparation of the gospel of peace, shield of faith, helmet of salvation, and sword of the spirit.*

During biblical times, a soldier would wear a wide *waist belt* that held his war weapons and his spoils. There were loops to hold his swords, ropes and even his darts. The belt was tied in several places to make sure it stayed in place so that no matter what obstacles the soldiers faced (moving around, falling down, climbing mountains, etc.) the belt was positioned, and the weapons were ready for the fight. If the belt was not on properly, then everything else would be out of place for the soldier, thus hindering his efficiency in battle and possibly costing him his life. As Christians, our belt of truth is the Word of God. Just as the soldier needs his loin belt to keep his armor together, we need the Word of God applied to our lives on a daily basis or we will not be able to maintain our defenses. Without it, we have no foundation on which to base our warfare with the enemy.

For a soldier, the *breastplate* protected the heart. It was designed to have ease of movement, but to also provide protection from blows. The heart is the one key organ responsible for sending blood through our circulatory system to keep us alive. Likewise, our spiritual lives can deaden if our hearts are not right with God. When you walk in the righteousness of God, it is a weapon of defense against all those slanderous accusations and outrageous strategies of the devil. Right thinking and doing right are the parts of righteousness with which we are to protect ourselves.

Historians have credited *footwear* as one of the greatest reasons why the Roman army was so victorious over its enemies. The Roman soldier was equipped with footwear that had spikes on the soles which provided them a strong stance and balance, giving them a superior posture in battles on hills and uneven terrain. The peace we receive from God will help us to stand with our feet planted firmly on the Word of God and to stay there unmoved by the devil's threats and lies. Peace will protect us when we walk through the rough places and keep us steady in the heat of a battle. Best of all, peace will keep our spiritual foes where they belong – under our feet.

Soldiers' *shields* often covered them from the chin to their knees. When groups of soldiers besieged a town, they would form circles by standing close together and holding their shield over their heads to protect the entire group from fiery arrows. In Ephesians 6:16, when it says *to take the shield of faith so that you are able to quench all the fiery darts of the wicked one* it is referring to the faith of the believer in the promises of God. The value of faith does not lie in the person exercising it, but rather in the God in whom we place our faith. Romans 10:17 tells us that *faith comes by hearing the Word of God.* Knowing the Bible and the God of the Bible gives us greater faith. We must always remember that it is God who fights with us, and protection does not get any better than that.

A well-designed *helmet* protects a soldier from various angles of attack. For Christians, one of the greatest battlefields is in our minds. This is the area that the enemy wants to attack the most. He wants to damage our assurance of salvation. Paul gave excellent advice in Philippians 4:8, *Finally, brethren, whatsoever things are true, whatsoever things are honest, whatsoever things are just, whatsoever things are pure, whatsoever things are lovely, whatsoever things are of good report; if there be any virtue, and if there be any praise, think on these things.* We must be on guard to monitor what we let run free in our minds. Satan has blinded the world in this area, and he will do the same to an unsuspecting or careless Christian. We must have a clear mind to be discerning in all situations, *which* comes by immersing ourselves in God's word and in prayer.

There are many types of swords, but there is one that is called a two-edged sword. Not only is this sword intended to kill, but also it can rip the enemy's insides to shreds. It cuts in two directions – going in and coming out. Paul describes the Word of God as our personal weapon or sword. When Jesus was tempted by Satan in the wilderness, He quoted his Father's words and spoke them with authority. Consequently, each word was like a sword-blow to Satan's head. God has given each of us the authority to use His word because we are all ambassadors of Christ. God has ultimate authority and when we speak His word, according to His will, we walk in that same power and authority.

After you have gotten dressed for battle – it is important that you not miss the next scripture in verse 18 of Ephesians 6, *Praying always with all prayer and supplication in the Spirit, being watchful to this end with all perseverance and supplication for all the saints.* We must be on alert and constantly in prayer. Don't let the enemy catch you slipping. Check your armor - do you have any cracks in it? Or are you fully dressed for battle?

## TOSS THE TEMPTATIONS

If you were on a diet, would you sit up with a triple chocolate cake with chocolate icing on your counter? No, of course not! Why would you want to tempt yourself by having something in which you could not indulge sitting right in front of your face? So why is it that we say we want to be free from the stronghold of pornography, yet we still have a subscription to Playboy? Why do we say we want to be free from masturbation, but we still have a dildo in our nightstand? Why do we say we want to abstain from sex, but he keeps a condom in his wallet and she stays on the pill, "just in case?" Satan doesn't have to tempt us because we make it easy for him by keeping the obvious temptations at arm's length.

One of the first things you must do now that you have made a commitment to abstain from all sexually immoral activity is to **clean house** and **toss the temptations.** Yes ladies, I understand that the pill helps your cramps – just take a Midol. Gentlemen, I know that you are carrying the condom "just in case," but why are you giving yourself an easy route to sin? Get rid of the condom and maybe in the time it would take you to go to the store to buy another one in the heat of the moment, you will remember your new commitment. And by all means, destroy the pornography, get rid of the sex toys, and anything else that has typically led you into sexual sin. For some, you may have to put away your Luther collection for awhile. For others, it may mean you have to cut out some R-Rated movies. For me, one of the many things I had to do was stay out of Victoria's Secret for awhile because if my underwear was too cute, I was going to want to show somebody. Over time, I've been delivered from that stronghold, and I can shop in Victoria's Secret again. I enjoy it for myself, with the understanding that one day MY HUSBAND can enjoy it too, but believe me, that didn't happen overnight. I had to go through a season of big, granny drawers until I got my flesh under control.

So think about all the things that "set the mood" for you. Think about the things that cause you to indulge in sexual activity. Think about the things that are temptations for you. I don't care what it is ...pack it away until you are stronger. Don't light candles when you have company if that is too much for you. Don't be foolish and think that you can handle something if you really can't. You have to know your weak points and be able to identify the traps. Also know that sometimes what sets you off may seem trivial, but in this critical time you can't take chances. I remember shortly after I made my commitment, I was at dinner on a date. Somewhere between finishing my appetizer and waiting for my main course, I got a whiff of his cologne (and all the ladies know that there is nothing like a good smelling man). All of a sudden, my mind went to a place that it had no business going. When I couldn't seem to gain control of my thoughts, I had to cut dinner short and call one of my girlfriends to pick me up from the restaurant. Yes, I felt like a fool explaining to this man that "I had to go," but the next morning when I woke up in my own bed, alone without the guilt of being entangled in someone else's sheets – it was all worth feeling foolish for a moment. And that is how radical you have to be sometimes.

Another important thing is to not compare yourself with others. What you can handle and what the next person can handle is not always the same thing, which is why you have to know yourself. Don't get caught up in someone giving you an eight-step remedy for how to abstain. That may have worked for them, but that may not be your story. Case in point, a wise woman told me, "Tanya, don't be at your boyfriend's house late at night. This will keep you from falling into sexual sin." These words may have been great advice for someone, but when I was having sex, time of day was not an issue. So yes, I was leaving his house before 9 PM, but that just meant we were having sex at 4 PM. Again, I say – you have to know yourself and what is a temptation <u>for you.</u> Hebrews 12:1 says *to let us lay aside every weight, and the sin which so easily ensnares us, and let us run with endurance the race that is set before us.* In other words – **TOSS THE TEMPTATIONS.**

---------------------------------------

So how do you feel? You have prayed a prayer of repentance, forgiven yourself, dealt with your disappointments, faced the facts, decided who was daddy, gotten dressed for battle and tossed the temptations. You have begun the process of being ARMED, thus making you a DANGEROUS threat to the enemy. There is no stopping you now. You are ready for war, and you can not be defeated. No one can condemn you or make you feel ashamed or guilty for your past because you have looked your sin in the eye. You have repented and turned away from your sinful ways. You are committed to living your life for Christ, you have put on the full armor of God, and you have gotten rid of those things (and people) who have been stumbling blocks in the past.

Now that you have done a little groundwork, you are ready for surgery. It may hurt a little - getting very intense as we pull off layer after layer of contamination from your temple. There may even be moments where you want to throw in the towel, but you have come too far now to turn back. You must finish the race – endure until the end.

Don't try to fight it or hold on to unhealthy habits, attitudes and mindsets. Let God renew your mind and your spirit. Remember, you are in the ICU so not everybody can be a part of this process. Get used to being alone sometimes. It doesn't make them bad people; it's just that where God wants to take you, not everyone can handle. Yet in the midst of it all, know this – God will never leave or forsake you, so you are never really alone.

Are you ready?

Are you open to whatever God has in store for you next?

Can you trust Him?

Do you really believe that you don't have to be<br>entangled in the bondage of sexual sin again?

Come on. The ICU is waiting for you ...

# CHAPTER 9: INTENSIVE CARE UNIT

You have been stripped, exposed and broken. If you are anything like me, your vulnerability may be trying to get the best of you right now because you are not used to standing naked before God. You either prefer that people think you have it all together all the time, or you just don't want to face the real you. Like Adam and Eve in the Garden of Eden after they ate the fruit from the forbidden tree, you may be trying to hide yourself under some "fig leaves" - but, you can't hide your sin from God. The facts are the same today as they were in the Garden of Eden – God already knows all about your sin. He is not surprised or blown away by your past. Believe me, you did not catch God off guard. As a matter of fact, He sent His son to die on the cross for your sin some 2000 years ago. He knew that you would find yourself entangled in sin, so He covered you in advance.

## WHAT IS THE PURPOSE OF THE ICU?

The ICU is the place of renewal, restoration and transformation.

**Renewal:**
To start over, to replenish, to make life new, to re-establish on a new and usually improved basis.

**Restoration:**
To put back together what has been torn or broken, to give new life or energy.

**Transformation:**
A marked change, as in appearance or character, usually for the better.

Upon entering this place of renewal, restoration and transformation – your attitude, mindsets, commitments, standards, and conduct all have to change. You will not leave here as the same person you were when you came. It's time for you to free yourself from your old habits and activities that fed your flesh and begin to feed your spirit. It's time for the "new man" to walk in the authority given by Christ. It's time for your life to line up with the commitment to *abstinence until marriage* that you have made. It's time that your "fruit" confirm whose team you are on and whose mandates you are carrying out. Remember, you decided that's He's your daddy, so now it's time to live for Him!

### Ephesians 4: 22-24

*Put off, concerning your former conduct, the old man
which grows corrupt according to the deceitful lusts,
and be renewed in the spirit of your mind, and that
you put on the new man which was created according
to God, in true righteousness and holiness.*

### Romans 12:1-2

*I beseech you therefore, brethren, by the mercies
of God, that you present your bodies a living
sacrifice, holy, acceptable to God, which is your
reasonable service. And do not be conformed
to this world, but be transformed, by the renewing
of your mind, that you may prove what is that
good and acceptable and perfect will of God.*

### Ephesians 5:8

*For you were once darkness, but now you are light in the Lord.
Walk as children of light.*

**Romans 6:18**

*And having been set free from sin, you become
slaves of righteousness.*

## ACCEPT RESPONSIBILITY

One thing that every Christian must do is begin to accept responsibility for his or her sin. Often we blame the devil for something that we have brought on ourselves. Romans 6:18 tells us that *we have been set free from sin, and have become slaves of righteousness.* So why are we still sinning? We continue to sin simply because we choose to be disobedient. No one is pulling our arm or forcing us to continue in sexual sin (or any other sin for that matter), but we like it and don't want to stop doing it.

It's like a child that has been told not to leave the front yard. There isn't anyone taunting him to leave the yard, but curiosity just gets the best of him - and off he goes. He heard his parents say to stay in the yard; he understood the rules and even the consequences. Yet he left the yard anyway – just being disobedient. Christians are the same way. We know what we are not supposed to do and the consequences of doing it – yet we choose to disobey.

Most of us are guilty of going into a situation saying, "I know this is wrong, but ..." Then we turn around and say that the devil made us do it. We give the devil entirely too much credit for the sin in our lives. It's time to step up to the plate and accept responsibility and make a decision not to continue in our sin of disobedience. I Peter 1:13-16 tells us to *gird up the loins of your mind, be sober, and rest in the hope fully upon the grace that is to be brought to you at the revelation of Jesus Christ; as **obedient** children, not conforming yourselves to the former lusts, as in your ignorance; but as He who called you is holy, you also be holy in all your conduct, because it is*

*written, "be holy, for I am holy."*

## STRIP

If you are ready to walk and live in total deliverance from your sexual sin, you must stand naked before God. Vulnerability and transparency are hardly easy, but you must stand boldly and allow Him to place a giant-size mirror in front of you and reveal the real you. To be vulnerable and transparent is an humbling experience. It takes you surrendering your will to God's perfect will. You have to relinquish the control you thought you had in and over your life and allow your creator to reconstruct you. When we walk around prideful, pretending to have all the answers, we will always miss the move of God in our lives. I Peter 5:5b says, *God resists the proud but gives grace to the humble.* The first step in stripping is to remove pride from our lives. Be completely transparent and see yourself for who you really are. Yes, I know that the good, the bad and the ugly are staring you in the face, but stay strong! Stay encouraged because a change is coming.

## EXAMINE YOURSELF

God wants you to be everything that He ordained for you to be when He formed you in your mother's womb. He's not breaking you to *hurt* you, but instead to *heal* you and make you whole again. God wants to strip your stuff off so that you can be transformed into His image. You've come to the right place, and you are in perfect hands.

You've already come a long way on this journey. You have faced a lot of issues that you may not have even realized were present in your life, and yet, you may find yourself still crying out to God about a "need" you have. You may think that the enemy is trying to throw certain things back in your face to get you off focus and to trip you up. It may be that you are not completely convinced that you can walk out your new commitment, but know that you can and you will. Acts 10:34 tells us that *God is no respecter of persons,* so if He did it for <u>me</u>, He will do the same for you. Now tell me, what is it my friend? What is tugging at your heart strings? What is it that you still feel you need from God? Be honest with yourself about the answer.

Do you need to be healed of the hurt and pain
left by emotional, physical or sexual abuse in your life?

Are you still holding on to the rejection from
someone you loved who left you after you slept with him or her?

Were you molested or raped and feel like you are in
prison because no one knows or understands what
you have been through?

Do you have a broken heart because someone
you trusted betrayed you?

Are you so absorbed in and addicted to masturbation
and pornography that only a touch from God can
destroy that stronghold?

Not knowing what it means to love and to be
loved, do you need to be taught by the creator of
love – the only one capable of loving unconditionally?

Are you afraid to love because you don't think you deserve it?

Do you need to forgive some people in your
life before you can move forward?

Do you need to gather the pieces of yourself that
you left with every person with whom you slept so
you can be made whole again?

Do you need your joy and peace restored?

Do you need to get over the guilt and shame of prostitution?

Do you still hear the cries of the baby you aborted
years ago, or the baby you had your girlfriend abort?

Are you dealing with the fact that you have a
sexually transmitted disease?

Whatever it is, **God is the answer.**

## IDENTIFY YOUR SUPPORT

God never expected you to do this on your own. He is your
strength and your support. Isaiah 43:1-2 says, *Fear not, for I have
redeemed you; I have called you by your name; You are Mine. When
you pass through the waters, I will be with you; and through the
rivers, they shall not overflow you. When you walk through the
fire, you shall not be burned, nor shall the flame scorch you.* Psalm
18:32 *says, It is God who arms me with strength and makes my way
perfect. He makes my feet like the feet of deer and sets me on my
high places.* And Deuteronomy 20:4 *says, for the Lord your God is*

*He who goes with you, to fight for you against your enemies, to save you.*

As you continue to identify the needs in your life, you may feel overwhelmed. You just have to continue to have faith that God can provide your *every* need. Know that He will meet you right where you are. Don't think that you have to get it all together first before you come to Him. As a matter of fact, you can't *get it together* without Him. You have to trust Him. God loves you so much, and His love is unconditional. He doesn't love like people love, based on who you are and what you do. He loves you in spite of everything you've done. How many people do you know are capable of loving you like that? His arms are outstretched, ready to embrace you. Will you let Him?

**Philippians 4:19**
And my God shall supply all your need according to
His riches in glory by Christ Jesus.

## CONNECT WITH GOD

You may be carrying hurt, disappointment, anger, guilt, shame, soul ties, lustful thoughts, etc., but God wants you to become intimate with Him so that He can remove those stains and replace them with His love, joy, peace, and spirit. Will you let him cleanse you? Will you willingly submit to this ICU experience? He is waiting for you. It's time for you to let go and let God.

Although our experiences may be different, there is one thing that remains consistent. On this journey, we all need GOD. We can't do it on our own. Think about it: you have probably tried to walk away from your sexual sins in your own strength time and time again and found that your strength was simply not enough. Invite Him in. He wants to walk with you. We stay so focused on the sin when instead we need to place our eyes on God and let Him deal with the sin. Matthew 6:33 says, *Seek first the kingdom of God and His righteousness, and all these things shall be added to you.* Stop worrying about your sin, and diligently run after God. Everything else will fall into its proper place. Let Him remove the things from your life that don't line up with His Word. Allow Him to remove the roots of your problems. No one can do it better than God.

### John 15:1-5
*I am the true vine, and My Father is the vinedresser. Every branch in Me that does not bear fruit He takes away; and every branch that bears fruit He prunes, that it may bear more fruit. You are already clean because of the word which I have spoken to you. Abide in Me, and I in you. As the branch cannot bear fruit of itself, unless it abides in the vine, neither can you, unless you abide in Me. I am the vine, you are the branches. He who abides in Me, and I in him, bears much fruit; for without Me you can do nothing.*

## THE PROCESS

What must happen here is simply between you and God. The ICU is a very personal process because each of us needs something different from God at this time, so I can't just give you some step-by-step remedy and expect it to be the perfect process for you. I can't completely walk you through this process; you have to totally

**trust God** to remove every layer of residue that your sexual past has created in your life. He knows your every hurt, pain and desire. He knows the situations with which you struggle. He knows what has you in bondage. He knows that *thing* that keeps you up late at night, all of which need to be addressed. Sexual addiction is like cancer: if the root of the problem is not handled and only part of the cancer is removed, it will continue to grow and spread and destroy the whole body.

Each of us has been affected differently by our sexual sins. We all have our own story and our own struggle. I could touch on 50 different topics and still miss your area that needs healing the most. For me, I had to first address my low self esteem. Then I had layers of baggage called anger, pride, shame, and disappointment that had to be peeled away. I also had unrealistic expectations for people: God had to show me that I was looking for a "perfection" in people that only He could provide. I had to humble myself and realize that I was not *"Super Woman"*, and so I didn't always have to appear like I had it all together.

For so many years, I thought that I had to be strong for everyone else, so I never took the time to tend to my own needs. There was so much "stuff" that had been building up inside that I had never addressed. So I experienced a **purging process** in the ICU. One by one, God and I addressed each issue by a series of topical studies. If the issue was fear, I grabbed my Bible and a Concordance and looked up and mediated on every scripture that dealt with fear until I could boldly say that I was FEARLESS because I found in II Timothy 1:7 that *God has not given us a spirit of fear, but of power and of love and of a sound mind.* If the issue was feeling overwhelmed or defeated, I reminded myself that in II Corinthians 4:8-9 it says, *we are hard-pressed on every side, yet not crushed; we are perplexed, but not in despair; persecuted, but not forsaken; struck down, but not destroyed.*

However, what I experienced on the surgery table in ICU isn't necessarily the same thing that you need, so I would be doing you a disservice by trying to just pass my ICU experience on to you. That's why you have to walk this part out on your own – just you and God. He knows where you have been, what you have suffered, and what you need to be completely delivered. As you identify those needs, find scriptures that deal with those needs. Study them, post them around your house, mediate on them, and believe them!

### Philippians 2: 12-13
Therefore, my beloved, as you have always obeyed,
not as in my presence only, but now much more
in my absence, work out your own salvation
with fear and trembling; for it is God who works
in you both to will and to do for His good pleasure.

## FIND YOUR TRUE IDENTITY

Relax. Your time in this place has been customized just for you. God has a plan and a purpose for your life that He wants you to fulfill. You were designed for a specific assignment, and He has already equipped you with everything you need to fulfill it - but you have to be committed to living your life for Him and completing your assignment.

# FROM PROMISCUITY
## To Proverbs 31

You also have to grab hold of who and what you really are. For years, you may have struggled with self esteem issues or just accepted less than you deserved for your life. You have to change your attitude and your mindset about yourself. It doesn't matter what anyone else told you or called you. What does God say about you? Genesis 1:27 tells us that *we were created in God's image.* Deuteronomy 28:13 tells us that *we are the head not the tail, and we shall be placed above only and not beneath.* Psalm 17:8 says that *we are the apple of His eye.* Romans 8:37 tells us that we *are more than conquerors.* Don't stop there. Take time to continuously search the scriptures for affirmation of who you are in Christ.

There is no better way to build your self esteem than to grab hold of what God says about you. You used to feed yourself toxins because you had a defeated attitude. You thought your past determined who you are today, but now you know as it states in I Corinthians 6:11 after a listing of different sinners it says, *and such were some of you. But you were washed, but you were sanctified, but you were justified in the name of the Lord Jesus and by the Spirit of our God.* Let go of your old identity. Mediate on scriptures that instill in you who you really are. Do this until you truly believe it. Then when old stuff tries to rise up, you have the ammunition to knock it right back down.

Pull down all the walls, take off the masks, and leave the facades that you have it all together behind you. Be encouraged. Stand steadfast. Seek His face like you never have before. Get in your Word and study all the scriptures that speak life to the dead situation in your life. Allow God to remove the contaminates that seek to destroy you. Take your prayer life to the next level. Submit your will to God's perfect will.

You have made it this far. Don't give up now
... Are you ready? You can do this ... I believe in you.

Watch the *master surgeon* transform your life. It's time for you to commune with God. You may not know how to begin this process. The options are unlimited: You may want to play a worship cd and begin to sing praise unto Him. Or if you play an instrument, you could play a sweet worship melody for Him. You can get a journal and write down what you are feeling. Or maybe you want to escape to the park and take in the pure essence of God through your surroundings: the birds chirping, the sound of the streaming water, the beauty of the clear skies, etc.

Whatever you decide to do – just go ahead and take that step. I promise that He will meet you right there. Take all the time you need to enter into His presence and spend some quality time with Him. Be still for a minute, stop talking and just listen to what He wants to share with you. Draw near to Him. There is a lot of work to be done in the ICU, so I challenge you to put down this book for a while as you seek His face in your own way. When you are finished in the ICU, I'll meet you with some final Post-OP Instructions and a commission for your life.

 CHAPTER 10: THE POST-OP INSTRUCTIONS

# FROM PROMISCUITY
## To Proverbs 31

Look at you! You made it through your "surgery." You opened your heart, mind and spirit up to God, allowing him to break, mold and rebuild you, and you are still standing. Regardless of what it took to get here, Praise God that you are here now! There is no looking back – it's forward motion only from here on out. Will it be easy? Probably not! Will you be tempted? Without a doubt! But every day you will grow stronger and stronger. Your commitment will in time become a natural part of your life. If you fall, don't stay down – get right back up and keep it moving. I am so proud of you. Remember that you can be *confident of this very thing, that He who has begun a good work in you will complete it until the day of Jesus Christ* (Philippians 1:6).

Thank you for allowing me to share both my past struggle with sexual immorality and my present victory in sexual integrity with you. This journey will last a lifetime because it is indeed an on-going process. Take this time as a single person to really learn the purpose for which God created sex and the roles and responsibilities that He has given Christian men and women regarding relationships and sex. Prepare yourself to be the husband or wife that He ordained you to be. The same level of commitment that it takes to abstain from sex until marriage is the same level of commitment that will be needed to abstain from infidelity when you get married. Sexual integrity is designed for everyone – single or married. Getting it right today prepares you for tomorrow. I just have a few final things to share with you before we say goodbye.

**TAKE YOUR SEAT**

Ephesians 2:1-6 says, *And you He made alive, who were dead in trespasses and sins, in which you once walked according to the course of this world, according to the prince of power of the*

*air, the spirit who now works in the sons of disobedience, among whom also we all once conducted ourselves in the lusts of our flesh, fulfilling the desires of the flesh and of the mind, and were by nature children of wrath, just as the others, But God, who is rich in mercy, because of His great love with which He loved us, even when we were dead in trespasses, made us alive together with Christ (by grace you have been saved), and raised us up together, and made us sit together in the heavenly places in Christ Jesus.* Simply put, **TAKE YOUR SEAT,** my friend. God has placed you in a seat of authority and the enemy is under your feet.

As long as you stay in your rightful position, you are covered and the enemy is defeated. God's hand on your life is like you standing under an umbrella in a rainstorm. You can see the storm all around you, but you stay dry as long as you stay under the umbrella. However, if you move out of your position or walk away from under the umbrella, you will become drenched by the rain or spiritually by the cares of the world. So stay in your seat!

## TAME THAT TONGUE

James 3:5-6 says, *Even so the tongue is a little member and boasts great things. See how great a forest a little fire kindles! And the tongue is a fire, a world of iniquity. The tongue is so set among our members that it defiles the whole body, and sets on fire the course of nature; and it is set on fire by hell.* Watch the conversations in which you engage. Don't leave the ICU and go sit around at dinner with your friends talking about sex. It only takes a little spark to ignite an entire forest fire. How many times have you heard on the news about someone's entire house burning down because they dropped one little lit cigarette in their bed? All it takes is *one* conversation in the wrong direction to steer you off the path of abstinence until marriage. Proverbs 15:4 says, *a wholesome tongue is*

*a tree of life, but perverseness in it breaks the spirit.* Your conversations need to be wholesome. Save the sexual conversations for you and your spouse. Why would you even want to tempt yourself by talking about something in which you can not engage?

You must also watch what you are putting into the atmosphere. No more defeated talk and *woe is me* mentality. I don't want to hear you say, "This is too hard, I can't do it." Remove that kind of dialogue completely from your vocabulary. If you keep telling yourself that you can't do it, then you won't. *Death and life are in the power of the tongue* (Proverbs 18:21). Which one are you speaking? Continuously speak life. Always encourage yourself. You *can* do this! You *will* exercise self-control and keep your commitment to abstinence. You are a *virtuous woman* of God or a *mighty man* of God. He has equipped you with everything you need for this fight. You are victorious in Him. Remember that you can do ALL things through Christ who strengthens you!

## SET SOME STANDARDS

You are in a position to re-set your standards or, in some cases, set a standard for the first time period. Don't set them on what the world says is okay because those ideals are not good enough. Your standard must be set by the Word of God. As a Christian, you only have one measuring stick and that is Christ Himself. Before making any decisions, find out what the scriptures say. The Bible is your final authority, so follow the instructions that you have been given.

Remember my original standard of not having sex before I graduated from high school? Had I used the Bible as my source of standards, I would still be a virgin because it clearly teaches us not to fornicate. What is my standard today? I Thessalonians 4:3-5, *For this is the will of God, your sanctification: that you should abstain from sexual immorality; that each of you should know how to possess his own vessel in sanctification and honor, not in passion of lust, like the Gentiles who do not know God.* Fornication or any form of sexual perversion is no longer an option.

It is important especially if you are not currently in a relationship, to set standards for yourself before entering into one. You need to be comfortable and confident in your commitment before getting involved with someone else. If you are already in a relationship, you need to make sure your partner shares your commitment, and that regardless of what has occurred up until this point, that you both set new standards. Don't ever allow another person to convince you to compromise your standards. If you meet someone, or are currently dating someone who can't respect the decisions you've made for your life, it's time to move on.

The Bible says in II Corinthians 6:14, *do not be unequally yoked together with unbelievers. For what fellowship has righteousness with lawlessness? And what communion has light with darkness?* I am convinced that this is not only talking about Christians not being yoked with non-Christians, but also referencing relationships, where you need to be linked with people who hold your same standards. We may both be saved, but if you are still comfortable with fornicating, I have no business dating you if I am committed to abstinence. And this stance is something that needs to be addressed early on. Don't wait until things get hot and heavy between you and your partner to address your commitment to abstinence. You need to have that discussion at the beginning before feelings get involved. It's easier to walk away after the first date than it is to walk away after the tenth one. So make your standards clear from day one.

## BE ACCOUNTABLE

You may be an independent person who thinks that you don't

need anyone, but the reality is that we all need someone to hold us accountable to our commitments. Take inventory. Who is in your inner circle? Do they share your commitments? One of the hardest things for me when I first decided to abstain from sex until marriage is that all my girlfriends were still having sex, which meant that I didn't have a support mechanism. And I needed someone who was going to call me at night and make sure I was in my own bed and *in it alone*. **Find some accountability partners.**

Make sure they are people with whom you can be open and honest. You have to be able to call them when you are tempted to make that "booty call" and know they won't encourage you to make it. Instead they will pray with you, or in more radical times, come keep you company to make sure you stay faithful to your commitment. After living by myself, I decided to have a roommate, which I know was God-ordained because she moved in around the same time that I made a serious commitment to abstinence. Having someone living with me immediately cut out having my boyfriend spending the night. And because she was also one of my accountability partners, I had to come home each night as well. Find you some friends who will truly walk with you. Proverbs 13:30 says *He who walks with wise men will be wise, but the companion of fools will be destroyed.* With whom are you walking?

If you look around and don't see anyone in sight who can hold you accountable, pray that God sends someone to you. He will. It may even be someone you least expect. God uses those who are discerning and will not allow you to fail. I remember one night while in college, I was *creeping* out of my apartment in the wee hours of the morning, and just as I grabbed my keys, my phone rang. I thought it was the guy whose house I was planning to visit (pre-caller id days), but when I answered, it was my college pastor. And all he said was, "Put down your keys, get back in your bed, and go to sleep." Talk about ruining the mood. I was messed up behind that call for months. It was awesome to me to know that God cared enough about little ole' Tanya to wake someone else up out of his sleep to call me and stop me from making a bad decision.

If you are in a relationship, make sure that you all are also accountable to each other. God has blessed me with a relationship with a man who shares my commitment. We not only honor our own vessels, but we honor each other's vessels. I don't want to do anything to make it hard for him to maintain his commitment, and likewise, he doesn't want to set me up to fail either. And we keep things real; there have been times when we just had to depart from each other's presence because flesh was trying to take over. There have been times when he has called me to go out and I knew that "my mind" just wasn't right - may have been a conversation I'd just had with a girlfriend or something I saw on TV, but my flesh was not under subjection at the moment. So you know what? I played it safe and stayed in ... by myself.

It's also important for others to hold you accountable *in* your relationship. If you are dating someone who none of your friends know, there's a problem. Who is holding you accountable? Don't give yourself that much credit to think that you can do this on your own. And that's not just about sex. Sometimes you just need an outside view of things because you know how we get when our "relationship blinders" are on. Psalms 1 says, *blessed is the man who walks not in the counsel of the ungodly, nor stands in the path of sinners, nor sits in the seat of the scornful; but his delight is in the law of the Lord, and His law he meditates day and night.* Make sure that whoever is holding you accountable is doing so based on the Word of God and not their personal opinion. It does not matter what they think, but rather what God says!

## GET OFF THE MILK

It's time to step up your game and really get into your Word. No more milk feedings – it's time for you to move to solid food. A year from now, I don't expect you to be in the same place that you are now. Get an understanding of the elementary principles and keep growing. You have to pursue your relationship with Christ like you used to pursue sexual relationships. Give Him your all.

You can't follow the instructions in the Bible if you don't know what they are. II Timothy 2:15 says, *be diligent to present yourself approved to God, a worker who does not need to be ashamed, rightly dividing the word of truth.* Webster's dictionary defines diligent as *marked by persevering, painstaking effort.* It sounds to me that it takes serious action to be diligent. You can't count on Wednesday night Bible Study and Sunday morning worship service to feed you! Do you only eat dinner twice a week? No - if you did, your physical body would deteriorate. And that is exactly what your spiritual body does when you don't feed it. In the first chapter of Colossians, Paul says that he is *praying for the brethren in Colosse that they be filled with the knowledge of His (God's) will in all wisdom and spiritual understanding; that they might walk worthy of the Lord, fully pleasing Him, being fruitful in every good work and increasing in the knowledge of God.*

Not only must you study your Word, but you must also increase your prayer life. I Thessalonians 5:17 says, *pray without ceasing.* Prayer is a strong weapon. When temptations come, you have to pray. When you feel discouraged and want to give up on your commitment, you have to pray. When the enemy tries to bring up your past, you have to pray. When you feel weak in your spirit, you have to pray. When you are trying to exercise self-control, you have to pray. Prayer keeps you alert, which means to be *vigilantly attentive or watchful.* Being alert is important because your adversary, the devil, walks about like a roaring lion, seeking whom he may devour. Don't let him catch you slipping!

## BE A LIGHT

For years, I influenced people to live a life of sin. Many people found themselves in compromising situations because they were following the path of destruction that I was living. I'm not sure how I came to be in a place of such influence and why people looked up to me and did the things I suggested or that I did, but it happened. If only I had been living a life for Christ instead of living a life that supported my flesh, I could have used my influence for good. Today, however, I am determined to be a light. We must obey Titus 2:3 and *be a teacher of good things.*

I ask you to remember that someone is always watching you, so make sure you are living a life that represents the God you serve. Think about this question: If they follow your lead, where will they end up? What are you teaching not just by your words, but by your actions? As Christians, we are to set the standards in the world - not be controlled by the world's standards. When people observe you, they should see something different than what they see in the world. When you walk into a room, does the atmosphere change or do you conform to the atmosphere?

Matthew 5:16 says, *Let your light so shine before men, that they may see your good works and glorify your Father in heaven.* Make sure your life is glorifying God. You were made in the image of God, so how are you doing in your representation of Him? Ephesians 5:1 says, *therefore be imitators of God as dear children.* According to Webster's Dictionary, to imitate means *to use or follow as a model, to copy the actions of, to appear like, to resemble or reproduce.* What will people see when they observe you?

For many, you will be the first encounter they have with

God. Will you be an invitation to Christ or a deterrent from Him? It's imperative that we bring the Word to life through our lives. We have all been commissioned in Matthew 28:19, *to go therefore and make disciples of all the nations, baptizing them in the name of the Father and of the Son and of the Holy Spirit, teaching them to observe all things that God has commanded you.* As you continue to grow in Christ and in your commitment, go back and grab your sister's and your brother's hand, and lead them from a life of sexual immorality to a life of sexual integrity. If we are to impact nations for Christ, it will take more of us stepping up to the plate and sharing the Gospel of Christ. Matthew 9:37 says, *the harvest truly is plentiful, but the laborers are few.* Are you going to keep your deliverance to yourself and just be excited that you are free from the stronghold of sexual immorality? Or are you going to do your part to build the Kingdom of God? Can God trust you with the commission to be fishers of men? I believe that He can. So **go ye therefore!**

------------------------------------

We have come a long way together, and now you are equipped and prepared to stand strong in God's strength. Walking this journey with you has caused me to renew my commitment as I am reminded that it's not about me anyway, but the assignment God has for my life. I love and support you, and I leave you with this final commission ...

### Our Commission

Society has defined for us what sexuality is and how we should conduct ourselves in our sexuality. The media has convinced us that anything goes, and we have believed this ideology and completely turned away from the original design of God.

Our magazines consistently teach us the "10 ways to keep your man" and "the 7 things your mom didn't tell you about love" and "the 8 ways to bring sizzle to the bedroom." The music lyrics encourage us to sleep around... "just keep it on the down low," and that "there is nothing wrong with a little bump and grind." The television encourages us to pursue as many sexual relationships as possible. Today's shows even tell us that it's okay to shack up, that gay and lesbian relationships are socially acceptable, and that pornography is a creative art form.

The world has completely perverted what God ordained to be beautiful.

**And the result ...**

Our families are falling apart, divorce is at an all time high, more of our teenagers are having babies, black women are leading the statistics of the number of persons infected with HIV, and our middle school students are having oral sex competitions and orgies on the school grounds. Yet we as **CHRISTIANS** are so concerned with simply getting our "praise" on, that we are sitting by as this destruction plays out right before our eyes.

We have let the enemy have authority in our lives for too long.

**BUT IT STOPS HERE.**

# FROM PROMISCUITY
## To Proverbs 31

We did not come to take sides. We've come to take over!

Let us stand together in the face of the enemy to declare that we are prepared to **Reign** and to **Rule.**

For we have been commissioned to **reveal** to the world what God says about sexuality, to **equip** others with the tools to maintain sexual integrity, and to **demonstrate** through our words and our lives what it means to be victorious in this area.

Our ultimate goal is to make sure every Christian is **ARMED** with the word of God, and practical application thus making him or her a **DANGEROUS** threat to the enemy.

# STUDY AND
# REFLECTION QUESTIONS

## CHAPTER 1: BACK TO THE BEGINNING
### *Low Self-Esteem: The Root of Self Destruction*

1. How has your definition of promiscuity changed?
2. What lies have Satan told you about yourself that you presently believe or have believed?
3. When you look in the mirror, what do you see in yourself?
4. There is life and death in the power of our tongues. Which one are you speaking?
5. If death, what are some scriptures that you can mediate on to begin building your self-value?
6. Are you making unhealthy decisions due to a need for acceptance by others?
7. Are your standards based on God's word or on popular opinion?
8. Do you love yourself?
9. What insecurities or fears do you need to give to God?

## CHAPTER 2: PROSTITUTION
### *Not Just A Street Mentality*

1. Has your idea of a prostitute or pimp been expanded?
2. How have you received payments for sex? Or how are you using sex to get something in return?
3. What negative statements has someone told you repeatedly that you now believe?
4. Do you believe that you have something other than sex to bring to the table?
5. What or by whom are you being controlled?
6. What baggage do you need to unpack?
7. Why or how have you justified your sexual sins?

8.  Are you ready to stop prostituting your temple?
9.  What changes do you need to make to properly posses your vessel in sanctification and honor?

## CHAPTER 3: PORNOGRAPHY & MASTURBATION
*Our Senses Magnified ~ Our Values Desensitized*

1.  What activities have you engaged in that contradicted what God created sex for?
2.  Are you feeding your flesh or your spirit?
3.  On what types of things do you constantly find yourself thinking?
4.  What needs to be erased from your mental video recorder?
5.  Make a list of the items in your house that need to be destroyed. What are you going to do about them?
6.  What extreme sacrifices do you need to make in your life?
7.  What conversations do you need to avoid?
8.  Have you asked God to renew your mind and spirit?
9.  What are some things you can do to increase your level of self-control?

## CHAPTER 4: CYCLES OF DESTRUCTION
*Searching For Love, Settling For Lust*

1.  Examine your life! Are you in a cycle of destruction?
2.  Are you mistaking lust for love?
3.  Who have you become "one" with? How can you destroy those sexual soul ties?
4.  How have you attempted to take fire into your bosom without getting burned? Meaning ... what games are you playing with consequences you think you are exempt from?

5. Have you become immune to values, boundaries, standards and morals?
6. What Godly advice are you giving out, but are not applying to your own life?
7. What is the flip side of your cycle of destruction?
8. What seeds are you sowing through sexual sin?
9. Are you abusing grace and mercy?

## CHAPTER 5: TWO FACES OF SALVATION
*From Freaky Fridays To Sunday Worship*

1. What double life have you been living?
2. Who do you really think you are fooling? Do you realize that God sees and knows everything?
3. Are your actions supporting the life you proclaim to be living?
4. What doors have you left open for the enemy to come back in through?
5. What do you need to do to stop straddling the fence and be 100% committed to living a life that's pleasing to God?
6. Are you ready to obey God's commandments and not continue to just run after his blessings and promises?
7. When will you stop saying "I'm sorry" and really "repent?"
8. What changes do you need to make in your life for a true transformation?
9. Would God receive you into His Kingdom today or vomit you out of His mouth?

## CHAPTER 6: FIGHTING FAMILIAR SPIRITS
*Change Of Mind Without A Change Of Heart*

1. Are you still returning to the very environments, situations and people you asked God to deliver you from?

2. What friends, habits, or activities do you need to change in order to keep this commitment of abstinence?
3. What other changes do you still need to make in your life?
4. How are you keeping your heart with all diligence?
5. What is your heart revealing about you?
6. Who is holding you accountable?
7. By whose standards are they holding you accountable- theirs or God's?
8. Do those in your inner circle even know about your commitment to abstinence?
9. How can you turn the passion that drives you to sex into a passion that will drive you to worship God?

## CHAPTER 7: DIVORCING SIN
*When Enough Is Finally Enough*

1. Have you gotten to the point where you are really ready to say *enough is enough?*
2. Is your heart, mind and soul made up to do it "God's" way?
3. Have you confessed your sins to God and asked Him to forgive you?
4. Do you really believe that you don't have to be entangled in the bondage of sexual sin anymore?
5. Have you tried to substitute *suppression for deliverance?*
6. Are you ready to be vocal about your commitment to abstinence until marriage?
7. Can you be real with yourself and identity your weak moments?
8. Are you ready to share your scars and testimony if God so leads you?
9. Are you open to whatever God has in store for you next?

## CHAPTER 8: THE PRE-OP PROCEDURES

1. Have you asked God to forgive you? Have you forgiving yourself?
2. Ask God to help you accept your past and move on.
3. Are you ready to stop passing blame and face the truths about yourself?
4. Can you destroy the skeletons in your closet so that no one else can use them against you?
5. Who's your daddy? Are you studying and applying His instructions to every area of your life?
6. Is there evidence (fruit) in your life that proves that God is your master?
7. What do you need to do to get dressed for battle?
8. What temptations are still staring you in the face, and what do you need to do to destroy them?
9. Are you ready to trust God?

## CHAPTER 9: INTENSIVE CARE UNIT

1. Have you done everything you needed to do to get naked before God? Or are you still wearing some masks?
2. Do you understand the purpose of the ICU?
3. Have you accepted responsibility for the choices you have made in your life?
4. Examine yourself and allow God to remove the root of every stronghold that continues to reign in your life.
5. Are you relying on God to provide the support and strength you need for this journey?
6. How do you commune with God?
7. What can you do to become more intimate with God?

8. Are you ready to look in the mirror and see the person that God sees when He looks at you?
9. Are you renewed, restored and transformed? If not, continue to seek God's face diligently. It's a process, but it will happen.

## CHAPTER 10: THE POST-OP INSTRUCTIONS

1. Have you given God praise for what He is already doing in your life?
2. Do you understand the seat of authority that you have been given? Are you ready to take your seat?
3. What are some areas in which you need to tame your tongue?
4. What are you putting into the atmosphere with your words?
5. Have you set new standards for your life? Re-evaluate them one more time to make sure them are set on God's word.
6. Who are your new accountability partners? Do you promise to be transparent with them?
7. Are you studying your word and praying more?
8. Are you being a teacher of good things- a true representation of the God you serve?
9. Are you ready to *go ye therefore?*

For more information or to correspond with Tanya Martin:

Armed & Dangerous

*Attention:*
**Tanya Martin**
P.O. Box 54003
Atlanta, GA 30308

*Email:*
tanya@themasterplan.biz

*Website:*
www.armedanddangerous.biz